BEACON HILL
SEAFOOD savoir faire

BEACON HILL SEAFOOD savoir faire

by
MARY
WAINWRIGHT
SULLIVAN

with illustrations by
Robert E. Kennedy

Sullivan, Mary Wainwright.
   Beacon Hill seafood.
   Includes index.
   1. Cookery (Sea food) I. Title.
TX747.S793   1977   641.6'9   77-12921
ISBN 0-914016-46-6

Printed in the United States of America
by Daamen Printing Company.
Design by A.L. Morris

CONTENTS

Part 1
THE MYSTIQUE OF BEACON HILL

Part 2
THE ART OF SEAFOOD COOKERY

FOREWORD

Cooking is often referred to as an art. To me it is a work of love, a pleasant concentration upon assembling ingredients, seasonings and condiments to come up with the most palate pleasing dish possible. The ability to use spirits, condiments, seasonings and herbs in their proper proportions—to complement and enhance, rather than mask and destroy the natural flavor of basic ingredients, is the art.

Fish and other seafoods are generally abused. Frying seems to be the ultimate of most cooks' experience with either. There are so many other ways to prepare and cook seafood. Most of them easy, quick and delicious.

Following are three primary rules to remember:

— Use fresh fish whenever possible. The fresher the better.
— Do not freeze seafood unless absolutely necessary. If purchased frozen—thaw quickly in running cold tap water and dry off well.
— Always drain off liquid of canned seafood unless contra-indicated in recipe.

I am particularly fond of fish and feel very fortunate to have spent most of my life in an area where seafood is plentiful, and to have lived in other parts of the country where many succulent seafood recipes have originated. You will find recipes from other countries in here which I have found most enjoyable, particularly those from England where I have spent considerable time with my daughter and her family. Many of the recipes in my forty year collection were obtained with considerable difficulty and cajoling.

I thank the many friends on whom my recipes were tried and who urged me to write my book, and the helpful folks who own the first edition and whose gracious notes have prompted this second revised edition. My present "fish man," Mr. Haley's son Dennis, owns the store which has been at the same location since 1892 and is now known as the Beacon Hill Seafood Market. I have traded there since 1934 and he keeps me abreast of the latest developments in the seafood business.

My appreciation also includes Bob Kennedy, one of Boston's leading artists, who did the illustrations for my *Beacon Hill Anthology*, many of which are included here. (The poetry in Part 1 is also excerpted from the *Anthology*, which was written in 1969 and published in 1974.) Bob has been an artistic historian of the old and new Boston for over a decade. A resident of Beacon Hill, he lives and works in an 1840 stable on Joy Street. My gratitude to my good friend Ursula Vincent who assisted in editing and proofreading my first edition.

Last but not least, I heartily thank the friends whose recipes I have used and have found delightful. I must admit, however, and with apology, that I have rarely accepted a recipe without making some change, addition, or deletion after trial.

I hope I have brought you a greater appreciation for, and a new found pleasure in successfully preparing and serving all seafoods. Bon Appétit!

Mary Wainwright Sullivan

Third Edition
February 1, 1987

PART 1

THE

MYSTIQUE

OF

BEACON

HILL

THE PAST . . .

An arched eyebrow on the face of Boston-town,
A warren of quaintness and charm,
Legend and reality closely bound,
A hill of great renown.

New England's aristocracy claimed it as their sod —
The Cabots addressing the Lodges
And the Lodges only the Lord!

After dusk the hill glowed in soft gaslight.
A maze of brick and cobblestone woven around Louisberg
Square in its cool and verdant setting resounded with
the whir of wheels bespoked and the rhythmic step of thoroughbreds.

Tales of Beacon Hill are many,
Told in poetry, prose and song.
The rich, the learned, the famed and infamous
Settled there ere long;
Sitting at the feet, as t'were,
Paying homage to those appointed to the Chair
In the gold domed seat of order, law and knowledge.

A tinkling hurdy-gurdy proclaimed each lovely Spring.
Hoops rolled through the Common made children's laughter ring.
Majestic trees vaulted the skies with pride.
Magnolia and white lilac adorned her as a bride.

Summer was a time for boating on the Charles,
For country trips and picnic jaunts . . .

In summer heat a quietness settled o'er the Hill
and one could hear the call of birds and the hum of bees
From garden to garden winging.
At the end of day—from the convent windows
Came sweet vesper voices singing.

The crisp Fall air rang with the voices of children
home from school, wading along through waves of
leaves all golden, red and brown.
The scent of roasted chestnuts was pungent on the air . . .
Mingling with the incense of wood fires burning whose
misty haze the Hill wore like a crown.

The harshest of seasons brought greatest renown,
For it was only at Yuletide that Beacon Hill opened her doors
to invite all Boston town.
People came from far and from near—
Strolling carolers gave joy to every ear.

A. McVoy McIntyre opens his *Beacon Hill—A Walking Tour**
with the following quote from Van Wyck Brooks: "There have been
books on the slope of Beacon Hill when the wolves still howled on
the summit."

He further related that in his great stone house at the top of
Trimountain John Hancock overlooked the Common. In 1775 men
such as John Singleton Copley, portraitist; William Scollay, apothe-
cary; Charles Bulfinch, architect; Jonathan Mason, merchant; Joseph
Woodward, shipowner; and Harrison Gray Otis, lawyer-politician,
comprised the nucleus which carved the face of Boston. Then the
China trade and the fishing industry produced an affluent New
England society which took over Beacon Hill.

Without fish it is doubtful that Boston would have become the
leading city in New England or that Beacon Hill would have developed at the turn of the nineteenth century into the architectural
gem it is today. Boston, with the largest pier in the world devoted
exclusively to fish, became the foremost fishing port in the western
hemisphere.

Accessible to the abundant cod grounds as well as a variety of
other seafood including excellent shellfish, both fishing and fish
have provided stable employment and nutritious food for Bostonians since the first colonist settled the seacoast. By 1794 eighty

---

*Available at The Bookstore, 76 Chestnut Street, Beacon Hill, Boston, Mass-
achusetts, 02108.

large wharves and innumerable warehouses crowded the harbor area
to handle Boston's growing sea commerce and fishing industry.

Shortly after the turn of the century New England's intrepid
sailors began to venture beyond the familiar West Indies and Euro-
pean ports to the east and set their sails for the Orient as they
developed the famous China trade. At the same time whaling and
cod fishery became great industries and the men who financed these
expeditions grew wealthy quickly.

The newfound wealth posed a problem, for these merchants and
shipowners sought a life style which scarcely existed in Boston at
that time. Perceiving a need for new housing land developers en-
larged the Beacon Hill section of Boston and laid out building lots
for those eager to settle there. Fortunately, Charles Bulfinch (the
foremost architect of that period) and Benjamin Asher (a devotee of
Bulfinch) were retained to custom design many of the handsome
homes of the Federal period which are standing today.

These new houses did not overlook the harbor, the site of the
merchants' businesses, but rather the placid Charles River and the
rolling hills beyond. Thus Beacon Hill became a place apart although
close to the busy waterfront.

From time to time fire destroyed some of the Beacon Hill
homes but they were quickly rebuilt, often exact duplicates of the
originals. Thus the past was preserved and recalls the time when
fishing, whaling, and the China trade provided the wealth which
built one of the city's finest residential areas.

PRESENT . . .

I know the Hill from poetry, song and story —
I knew her when she stood out in her glory,
But fate has been unkind t'would seem . . .
Her glory now a shattered dream.

One season like the other — except for warm or cold —
Her fame now of another ilk . . .
On with the new — off with the old!

The Hill is often referred to as "a rabbit warren of streets" homogenous in character, yet one will observe several types of architecture: Federal, English Georgian, Greek Revival, Victorian, and today, incongruous bits of modern architecture. It is delightful to find yourself in the middle of Louisberg Square, and if you have visited London, feel yourself transported to Belgrave. Again, when you raise your eyes to the lovely lacy ironwork across the front of so many of the Hill houses, the view recalls Le Carré Français in New Orleans.

With its brick sidewalks, few remaining cobbled streets, and soft gaslights, in spite of present day hustle and bustle, residents and visitors experience both pride and pleasure. Although the Hill is famous for its homes, Charles Street, its only business thoroughfare at the foot of the slope, is equally renowned for its fine antique shops, ethnic restaurants, and other stores. These include flower shops, ice-cream emporiums, a hardware store, drug stores, grocery stores, beauty shops, Miss Lucy's—a quaint candy shop, a pet shop, artisan shops, and the business which probably predates all the others—the Beacon Hill Seafood Market—soon to celebrate its one hundredth anniversary. Another business landmark is Brigham's Provision, a block from Charles Street. The oldest market in Boston, it occupies the first floor of a building that is over two hundred years old.

On a summer's night at the foot of the Hill small sailboats line the shore of the Charles, a perfect setting for the popular Arthur Fiedler concerts. Above, the Public Garden offers a welcome oasis with its furry and winged friends and stately swan boats. Nearby in Boston Common the Frog Pond provides another summer refuge and becomes a skaters' delight in the winter. All this bespeaks the charm of a past which it is hoped will forever be preserved beneath the gold domed capitol.

Many people associate baked beans rather than fish with Saturday night dining in Boston. It is the seafood, however, which attracts visitors to the city's gourmet restaurants. Most Bostonians take their seafood for granted since the harvest of the sea is so close at hand and of such unfailing quality. Doubtless in the early 1800s when the Otis, Higginson, Swan, or Amory-Ticknor families entertained in their newly constructed homes on Beacon Hill, their cooks used old recipes for the delectable seafood they served. These same recipes, in turn, have been passed down from generation to generation and shared with others over the intervening years. Today many residents of the Hill enjoy the time-tested recipes, many of which are included in this book.

FUTURE . . .

There is still some vestige of past glory remaining —
Upheld by a few vigorous souls on the Hill.
The hope of her future lies with these who are
working at odds with patience and will
to hold on to some semblance of olden charm —
Who haven't succumbed to the breaking apart
of the cobblestoned Hill that was once Boston's heart!

'Tisn't sharing the Hill that upsets one the most —
It's something more than that.
Of her quaintness and charm you'll still hear boast —
Yet there are those who find Her simply old hat!

I look to the future — to a saving grace that will
comb out the snarls and wash her face . . .
Befitting a lady of her years — once more give her
pride and dignity — allay her fears and let her
look out as before on a town that will love her for evermore!

PART 2

THE

ART

OF

SEAFOOD

COOKERY

A FEW SUGGESTIONS

Buy fish in season when it is abundant, at its best, and less expensive. Your local fish market is the best source of information on this score.

Select fish whose fins are stiff, scales bright, flesh firm, with eyes clear and bulging. The gills should be pink, clean, and fresh smelling. The flesh should spring back when pressed. There should not be a strong odor, however, thoroughly clean and wash in several waters before cooking.

Plan on approximately ⅓ to ½ pound per person, or 1 pound of whole fish per person—do not count bones, head, or tail in purchased weight.

Fish breaks down very easily. As soon as it comes from the market place it in a covered dish in the refrigerator. Do not thaw frozen fish at room temperature. Either cook without thawing, as some recipes indicate, or thaw under running cold tap water and dry off before cooking.

Overcooking is the greatest and most usual offense. Too much or too long cooking robs fish of its flavor and dries it out. Start testing by flaking with a fork or toothpick after the first 7-10 minutes of cooking—sooner if pieces are very thin.

FISH FACTS

Fish and shellfish are high in nutritive value and relatively low in cost. Too, they are easy to cook, and add a variety to your meals.

Sticks — Elongated pieces of fish cut from fillets and steaks.

Fillets — The side cut of fish. They are lengthwise pieces of fish which are practically boneless and have very little waste.

Steaks — Cross section cuts of dressed fish which are about ¾ of an inch thick.

Dressed and Cleaned — Entrails and scales are removed from dressed fish. Most dressed fish have the head, fins, and tail removed also. These are ready to cook as bought.

Drawn — Fish that has been eviscerated. Scales, fins, and tail have been removed.

Whole or Round — Fish just from the water. To prepare for cooking the scales, entrails, head, fins, and tail must be removed. Some small fish are cooked without removing the fins and tail.

The following table suggests the right amounts of fish to buy:

Fresh or Frozen	*Amount per person*
Fillets or sticks	6-7 oz. each
Steaks	½ lb. each
Dressed fish	¾ lb. each
Whole or round fish	1 lb. (before preparing)

SHELLFISH FACTS

You can buy shellfish in various forms. Know the market forms and how to buy when you shop.

Cooked Meat — The edible portion of the shellfish removed from the shell after it is cooked.

In Shell — Shellfish can be purchased still in the shell. Hard and soft blue crabs, clams, lobsters, and oysters should be alive when bought in the shell unless already cooked in the shell. Lobsters and crabs can be cooked in the shell before marketing.

Headless — Shellfish with their heads removed before marketing, such as shrimp and lobster.

Shucked — Meat from clams, oysters, and scallops which has been removed from the shell.

The following table suggests the usual quantities required to serve six people:

		To serve 6
Crabs — Hard or soft — Live		6-12 lbs.
		(18-36 crabs)
	Cooked Meat	1½ lbs.
Lobsters — Live		4-6 lbs.
	Cooked Meat	2 lbs.

Oysters and Clams — In shell	5 dozen
Shucked	1½ qt.
Scallops — Removed from shell	2 lbs.
Shrimp — Headless, fresh or frozen	2 lbs.
Cooked Meat	1½ lbs.

COOKING WITH HERBS

Seafood has such a delicate flavor of its own that unlike many other foods it usually does not need herbs to bring out its true taste. A few of the more common herbs are included in some of the recipes which follow.

Most herbs come in containers with some direction as to their use. Nearly all of the herbs mentioned can be easily grown or bought. They may be used fresh, dried, or frozen. When dried they have about twice the strength of fresh. To dry, harvest herb when plant first flowers. Dry in an airy room and store in airtight containers in a cool dry place.

I will begin with two important DON'Ts: Don't spoil a dish by using an herb you are not familiar with or do not have directions for its use; Don't confuse herbs with seasonings. The secret in using herbs successfully is to use them SPARINGLY, some more sparingly than others, as further indicated. Most herbs bring out the natural salt in foods—others add to the salty flavor, but one can curtail use of salt when using herbs, which is more healthful.

Overuse of herbs, spirits, condiments, or seasonings will ruin the best recipe. Remember, some seafoods such as quahogs, clams, and other saltwater fish need little or no salt, and that includes the salt herbs. Herbs, when used, bring out the natural salt in foods. Butter, lemon juice, parsley (fresh or dry flaked), sweet or sour cream, and a modicum of wine or other spirits enhance the flavor of some fish, but just salt and pepper are generally adequate. Melted butter and parsley, with a little lemon juice, make a delicious sauce for poached, fried, or baked fish. Slices of fresh lemon and sprigs of fresh parsley are the best garnishes for broiled or baked fish. Fresh watercress is fine when you can get it.

The herbs I have found best for seafood cookery include the following:

Chervil — Of the parsley family, it is good in butter sauce or with cheese omelet. Used fresh, it makes a garnish for salads and grilled fish.

Dill — Best known as a flavoring for vinegar and pickles. Fresh sprigs go well with fish.

Fennel — This feathery herb is excellent in fish sauce and salad dressings.

Parsley — Fresh—it is the best known garnish for meat, fish, vegetables, potato salad, and canapés—full flower or finely chopped. Dried, use as flavor for sauces, soups, and stews.

Saffron — Delicious in chowders or fish soups. Use more sparingly
than all other herbs.
Tarragon — Excellent in cooking raw shellfish.
Thyme — Warm in butter and serve with lobster, prawns, and
shrimp. It can make fancy fare of the lowliest dish.

In combining herbs, pick your combinations of taste with
care—to complement your dishes—without individual
domination—without masking the natural flavor of what you are
preparing. The delicacy of flavor of whatever you are cooking should
determine the amount you use of any herb.

An aromatic flavoring which makes most foods and beverages
excitingly different, along with herbs, is angostura bitters.

If you have not heard about the "Romance of Angostura Bitters" send for it from the address on the bottle. Bitters may be purchased at grocery stores as well as shops that carry only "spirits." One
thing the book does not emphasize, however, is that bitters *must* be
used very sparingly to be effective. One to three drops go a long way.
Two drops in a cup of black coffee after dinner are delicious and your
guests will praise your "new and different coffee" if you keep it a
secret. You will find it in many of my own recipes.

WINES BEST SERVED WITH SEAFOOD

*"When a man drinks wine with dinner, he begins to be better
pleased with himself."*

Plato

Writing today, Plato might have added that man tends more and
more to drink the wine that pleases his personal taste rather than
follow the dictates of the connoisseur—as well he should. Nonethe-
less, white wines and rosés, by tradition and common sense, are best
with seafood. The red wines tend to overpower the delicate and
lightly seasoned flavor of virtually all dishes based on fish or any of
its briny counterparts, however prepared.

If your pocketbook permits and your palate agrees, the estate-
bottled vintage wines of France are unsurpassed, and a good champagne complements any fish. I personally find a white Bordeaux and
Graves excellent and a white Burgundy always good, but there is a
host of fine, imported white wines to choose from, some still relatively inexpensive.

Domestic wines have an equal interest for the seafood chef who
wishes to turn a gourmet meal into an occasion. California is the
largest producer of wine in the United States and the best of these
vintages comes from the Napa Valley. California owes its preemi-
nence not only to the Spanish missionaries, but to a bizarre and
extravagant Hungarian Colonel, Count Agoston Haraszthy, who

about one hundred years ago persuaded the state government of California to give him a blank check to buy vine stocks in Europe. He shipped back more than 200,000 cuttings and rooted vines of 1,400 varieties, among them the great Burgundian Pinot, Cabernet, Sauvignon, and Semillon species from Bordeaux, Riesling from the Rhine, Sylvaner and Traminer from Alsace, and even the Loire's Chenin Blanc. Wine being produced in California today is a good deal more like the Italian original than that made from French and German varieties.

California, however, is but one of the twenty-seven states which produce wine commercially, much of it very good indeed. New York State's grape belt along the Hudson Valley, the border of Lake Erie and the Niagara River, in the Finger Lakes district, and along the southern shores of Lake Ontario, produces fine wine. Much of the white wine produced from these regions will do regal justice as an accompaniment to the recipes in this book.

The prescription is really quite simple. Experiment and determine what you really like. Just be sure to stay with the white wines—rosés if you must—and chill thoroughly before serving. À votre santé!

FISH ENTREES

CREAMED CODFISH
(Dennisport, Massachusetts)

1 cup salt codfish
1 cup thin white sauce
1 hard boiled egg
¼ tsp. pepper
Pinch of fennel

Freshen fish by letting stand in water at room temperature overnight. Throw off water and place in fresh water and simmer for about 5 minutes or until fish is tender. Drain and add to white sauce with seasoning. Improves with sitting in refrigerator. Reheat and serve with baked or boiled potatoes. Sieve egg over creamed fish. Serves 2-3.

GRILLED POMPANO
(Florida)

Coat pompano (or sole) on each side with mayonnaise and sprinkle with seasoned salt and lemon pepper. Cook under broiler, or on outdoor grill, until mayonnaise is bubbly and golden.

BACALHOU
(New Bedford, Massachusetts)

1 lb. dry salt cod
4 med. potatoes
2 eggs—hard boiled
2 med. onions
½ cup olive oil
1 tsp. parsley flakes
1 doz. pitted black olives
2 tbsps. butter
Pepper to taste
2 tbsps. wine vinegar
1 clove of garlic, crushed
2 tbsps. milk

Cover cod with water and bring to boil and throw away water, repeat and let stand in cold water until ready to use. Sauté onions in olive oil with garlic until transparent. Boil potatoes and when done cut in slices, reserving one to be mashed with butter and fluffed for topping. Slice eggs and arrange in buttered baking dish. Arrange layers of fish, egg, sliced olives, and potato, pouring a little of oil and onion mix until all ingredients used up. Sprinkle pepper, parsley and wine vinegar over all. Top with fluffed mashed potatoes and place in oven at 350 degrees until top browns. Serves 6-8.

BARBECUED BASS
(Texas)

*3 to 4 lb. bass, cleaned and
ready for cooking
Salt (amount depends on
whether fresh or salt water
bass)
2 tbsps. chopped onion
1 tbsp. butter
1 cup catsup
3 tbsps. Worcestershire sauce
2 tbsps. brown sugar
2 tbsps. wine vinegar
¼ cup lemon juice
⅛ tsp. pepper*

Place fish in buttered shallow pan; sprinkle with salt. Sauté onion in butter until golden; add catsup, Worcestershire sauce, sugar, ¼ teaspoon salt, vinegar, lemon juice and pepper. Simmer 5 minutes and pour over fish. Bake at 425 degrees 35-45 minutes depending on size of fish. Serves 6-8.

JOE'S BROILED SEA BASS

2 lbs. of bass fillets
½ cup wine vinegar
2 tsps. garlic powder
¼ cup chopped parsley

Brush fish with vinegar. Sprinkle all sides with garlic powder and some chopped parsley. Broil 4 inches from unit for about 8 minutes, basting with vinegar frequently. Serve with vinegar sauce (mix 3 tablespoons chopped parsley with ¾ cup wine vinegar). Serves 4.

BEACON HILL CAPER

2 lbs. cod fillets
½ tsp. onion salt
½ tsp. paprika
½ tsp. nutmeg
½ tsp. mace
1 tbsp. capers
1 lime sliced
2-3 dashes Angostura Bitters
(optional)

Cut cod in strips about 1½ inches by 3 inches. Place in lightly buttered, shallow, baking dish. Combine onion salt, paprika, nutmeg, and mace. Sprinkle over fish. Add capers. Place lime over fish and sprinkle with Bitters. Bake at 400 degrees for 8 minutes or until fish flakes easily with fork. Serves 6.

CAPE COD TURKEY
(Old New England)

4 lbs. haddock or cod
1 cup of salt
¼ lb. salt pork
3 hard cooked eggs
¾ cup melted butter

Split, clean, and wipe fish. Remove tail. Sprinkle inside with salt and let stand in refrigerator overnight. Next day rinse thoroughly, removing salt. Tie in cheese cloth and simmer in water gently about 30 minutes or until tender and flaky. Place fish on platter after removing cloth and surround with boiled even-sized small potatoes and small buttered beets. Pour egg sauce* and salt pork scraps over fish. Garnish with fresh parsley. Serves 6.

---

*Egg Sauce: Chop eggs and add to melted butter. Fry out diced salt pork until golden and add to eggs and butter.

COD CUTLETS BRETONNE

4 large cod steaks
Juice of one lemon
Salt and pepper to taste
¼ pt. of dry cider (white
wine can be used)
5 tbsps. water
1 med. size carrot
1 med. size onion
2 sticks of celery
1 oz. of butter
1 tbsp. flour
2-3 tbsps. light cream
1 tbsp. chopped parsley

Wash and dry fish. Sprinkle with lemon juice and salt and let stand 30 minutes. Dab away excess liquid and place in buttered baking dish. Pour half of cider and water over fish and poach for 10-15 minutes in oven at 350 degrees. Shred vegetables into a small pan with nut of butter and remaining cider. Cover tightly and cook over medium heat 2-3 minutes and then place in oven. Take up fish, remove center bone and any skin and put on hot serving dish. Strain liquid and add rest of butter and flour mixed to a paste—simmer gently and add cream and parsley (sauce should be creamy), pour over fish and vegetables and serve. Serves 4.

BROILED FILLETS CONTINENTAL
(British Columbia)

1 lb. fish fillets
Salt and pepper to taste
Juice of ½ lemon
3 tbsps. butter
3 small onions, sliced thin
½ cup dry white wine
1 tbsp. flour
½ cup milk
¼ cup sliced stuffed olives
Pinch of saffron

Place fillets on preheated buttered broiling pan. Sprinkle with salt, pepper and lemon juice. Arrange onion slices over fish. Dot with butter. Broil 3 inches from unit, basting frequently with wine—for 10 minutes, or until fish flakes easily. Arrange fish and onion slices on a hot platter. Melt 1 tablespoon of butter in saucepan, blend in flour. Add liquid in broiling pan; combine with milk and gradually blend into flour mixture and cook gently until thickened and smooth. Stir in olives. Pour sauce over fish. Serves 3-4.

CUTTYHUNK FISH STEAKS

6 halibut or cod steaks
1 cup prepared mustard
⅔ cup tomato juice
¼ tsp. garlic powder

Combine mustard, tomato juice, and garlic until even consistency. Spread on both sides of fish steaks. Bake at 400 degrees for 12 minutes. Serves 6.

BAKED EELS
(Westport Harbor, Massachusetts)

Grease a large baking dish and place a rack in it. Slice eel in 1½-2 inch pieces and roll in flour. Alternate slices with slices of raw potatoes in rows on rack. Potatoes can be omitted. Place slices of raw bacon on top. Bake in 350 degree oven for 45 minutes—if potatoes used, until they are done.

CHEDDAR FILLETS
(Frankie's)

*2 lbs. pollack or cod
(or haddock)
1 tsp. minced onion
4 tbsps. butter
4 tbsps. flour
2 cups milk
1 cup grated cheddar cheese
2 carrots grated
Bread crumbs
1 tsp. parsley flakes
Just a few fennel seeds*

Grate onion on fish and place in double boiler. Cover tightly and cook until fish flakes easily with fork. Place fish in greased casserole. Make white sauce—melt butter in saucepan, add flour and blend—add milk stirring constantly and cook gently until thickened. Add grated cheese and carrot, parsley and fennel—pour sauce over fish and top with buttered crumbs. Bake at 350 degrees until golden brown—about ½ hour. Serves 4-6.

FILLET FOLLY
(Moi)

6 small fillets
1 lemon
Salt and pepper to taste
2 tbsps. chopped chives
2 tbsps. minced parsley
1 small onion–chopped
½ cup beer

Butter deep muffin wells, roll fillets and stand in wells after sprinkling one side with lemon and seasonings. In small saucepan melt butter and add onion and sauté until tender; add beer and bring to boil, remove from heat. Pour over center of fillets and bake at 375 degrees for 20 minutes. Serves 4-6.

HOLIDAY BRUNCH FILLETS

1 lb. flounder fillets
1½ tbsps. lemon juice
2 tbsps. soy sauce
⅛ tsp. cayenne pepper
Melted butter seasoned with
a pinch of fennel

Prick fish all over with fork. Combine lemon juice, soy sauce, and cayenne pepper and pour over fish. Marinate for 30 minutes. Bake at 400 degrees for 8 minutes or until fish flakes easily. Serves 4.

FILLETS MEUNIERE

4 fillets of your choice
Flour
4 tbsps. butter
Salt and pepper to taste
Chopped parsley
Juice of one lemon

Dredge fillets with flour and brown in butter on both sides. Turn them gently with spatula being careful not to break them. Be sure your heat is low and cook gently until flaky with fork. Test on edge. Season with salt and pepper. Remove to a hot platter. To pan juices add lemon juice and parsley and stir over low heat. Pour over fillets and serve with lemon wedges. Serves 4.

CRISPY CRUMB FILLETS

2 slices of whole wheat bread
¾ lb. fillets (sole, halibut, or
flounder)
1 tsp. parsley flakes
¼ cup milk
½ tsp. tarragon

Dry bread and crumble; add parsley and tarragon. Dip fish into milk, then into crumbs, coating well on all sides. Place in lightly greased pan. Gently pour any remaining milk over fish and bake at 400 degrees for 10 minutes and serve with tart sauce (See sauces). Serves 2.

FILLET OF FISH BAKED WITH HERBED CRUMBS
(Canada)

1½ lb. filleted fish
Salt to taste
6 pats butter
3 cups of soft bread crumbs
¼ tsp. whole marjoram
leaves
¾ to 1 tsp. salt
¼ tsp. black pepper
⅓ cup melted butter

Cut fish into 6 serving pieces. Place in a buttered 9 inch baking pan. Sprinkle each piece with a dash of salt and a pat of butter. Mix remaining ingredients and sprinkle uniformly over fish. Bake in a preheated moderate oven 350 degrees—25-30 minutes. Serves 6.

DANISH FISH FILLETS

2 tbsps. minced onion
¼ cup chicken bouillon
1 cup tomato juice
½ cup chopped cucumber
¼ tsp. dill
2 tsps. sugar
Dash of pepper
1 lb. fish fillets of your choice
Lemon slices for garnish

Cook onion in bouillon until soft. Add tomato juice, cucumber, dill, sugar, and pepper. Bring just to boil and simmer 10 minutes, stirring constantly. Place half of the sauce in shallow baking dish—arrange fillets on sauce—pour remaining sauce over fish and bake 20 minutes at 400 degrees. Serves 2.

GRILLED SWORDFISH
(Barbecue Sauce)

2 lbs. fresh swordfish
½ cup soy sauce
4 tbsps. tomato sauce
2 tbsps. lemon juice
¼ cup chopped parsley
1 tsp. powdered oregano
½ cup orange juice
1 tsp. fresh ground pepper
1 garlic clove

Mix soy sauce, chopped garlic clove, tomato sauce, lemon juice, parsley, oregano, orange juice, and pepper. Soak swordfish in mixture for 2 hours in refrigerator, before cooking. Place in greased wire broiler, grill over medium hot coals 5-8 minutes. Baste with mixture and turn—broil 5-8 minutes longer.

The same effect can be accomplished with your stove broiler; just add a little liquid smoke or hickory seasoning to mix. Serves 4.

HALIBUT FIORENTINA
(North End, Boston)

4 10-oz. halibut steaks (cod
or flounder)
Salt and pepper to taste
¾ cup chicken bouillon (or
clam juice)*
¼ cup wine vinegar
2 tbsps. finely chopped
parsley
1 small clove garlic, minced
½ tsp. oregano leaves

Sprinkle fish steaks with salt. Place in pan. Combine remaining ingredients, pour over fish and marinate in refrigerator for 3 hours. Drain and reserve marinade.

Broil on rack about 4 inches from source of heat for 8 minutes or until fish flakes easily with fork. Baste with marinade several times during broiling; turn once after 4 minutes, carefully. Serves 4.

_____

*If clam juice is used cut down on salt.

BAKED SCROD*
(Boston)

4 fish steaks approx. 10 oz. each
½ tsp. celery salt
Salt and pepper to taste
¼ cup onion flakes
1 tsp. butter
1 cup of milk
2 tsps. minced parsley

Sprinkle fish with seasonings and place in baking dish. Sprinkle with onion flakes. Combine butter, milk and parsley and slowly pour ½ of this mixture over fish. Bake at 350 degrees for 10 minutes. Slowly pour remaining milk mixture over fish and bake added 10 minutes or until fish flakes easily with a fork. Serves 4.

---

*A young cod, split down the back, and backbone removed, except a small portion near the tail, is called a scrod. Haddock is also so dressed.

FILLETS DE SOLE AU CHAMPAGNE

12 small fillets of sole
1 pint of brut champagne
1 tbsp. flour
½ cup butter
2 egg yolks
1 med. onion thinly sliced
Salt and pepper to taste
1 lemon

Salt fish on both sides. Butter a casserole dish. Place onions around bottom and place fillets on top. Add champagne. Bring to gentle bubble at 325 degrees, let bubble gently for 10 minutes.

Make roux: Melt butter, add flour, and strain juices fish cooked in and add to roux and beat vigorously with wire whisk. Beat in egg yolks and reheat gently for 1 minute stirring constantly. Add a few drops of lemon juice and taste for seasoning. Place fish on hot platter and pour sauce over fillets—covering. This dish may look difficult, but is not, it just requires your full attention. Preparation time 20 minutes. Cooking time 10 minutes. Sauce 10 minutes. Serves 6.

EELS EXTRAORDINAIRE
(North End, Boston)

Cut eels into ½ inch slices and dip in cracker meal. Fry in vegetable oil until golden brown. Make a lemon sauce with ½ tablespoon cornstarch, ¼ cup water and 3 tablespoons lemon juice. Cook to thicken and pour over fried eels.

CRUNCHY BROILED FISH

1 ½ lbs. fish fillets
¼ cup cooking oil
Juice of one lemon
½ cup cornflakes, lightly rolled
3 tbsps. chopped parsley
1 tsp. salt
½ tsp. paprika
Melted butter

Cut fillets into individual serving pieces. Roll in mixture of oil and lemon juice, then in cornflakes, parsley and seasoning. Place on greased baking sheet and broil 3 inches from unit—5 minutes if ½ inch thick—8-10 minutes for 1 inch thick. Baste several times with melted butter. Makes 4-6 servings.

FLOUNDER NAPOLEON
(The Colony Club)

1 lb. flounder fillets
½ tsp. salt
⅛ tsp. pepper
⅛ tsp. garlic powder
¼ cup sliced mushrooms
¼ cup chicken bouillon
2 tbsps. parsley flakes
1 small tomato, diced

Sprinkle flounder with salt, pepper and garlic. Place in shallow baking dish and add mushrooms. Combine bouillon and parsley flakes and pour down sides of baking dish. Bake at 375 degrees for 12 minutes. Serve topped with diced tomato. Serves 2-4.

ROSEMARY SALMON
(For your fall cookouts)

2 lbs. fresh salmon steaks
2 tbsps. lemon juice
¼ cup salad oil
½ tsp. dried rosemary leaves
crushed
Salt and pepper to taste

Mix oil, lemon juice, and rosemary together. Shake well. Let stand at room temperature 1 hour. Strain. Cut fish in 4 portions. Dip into oil mixture, sprinkle with salt and pepper. Place in medium greased wire broiler. Grill over medium hot coals 5-8 minutes (depending on thickness). Base with oil mixture and turn, grill 5-8 minutes more. Do *not* over cook.

The same effect can be accomplished with your stove broiler, just add a little liquid smoke to the oil mixture, or shake a little hickory seasoning on fish. Serves 4.

SAUMON AU VIN BLANC
(le Touraine, France)

Gaelic version of the American 4th of July salmon-and-peas, why not serve "saumon au vin blanc" with "petits pois à la française"?

4 salmon steaks
Butter
Salt and pepper to taste
1 cup of white wine
(Vouvray perferred)
Steamed potatoes (over salted water)
Green peas, fresh if available

In a heavy skillet brown steaks in plenty of butter. Add salt and pepper, when salmon is half cooked, pour in wine. Simmer over a brisk flame until the butter and wine are reduced to a rich but still juicy sauce. Serve with steamed potatoes and French peas.* Serves 4.

---

*French Peas: In covered pan, with low flame, simmer 2 cups of green peas in ¼ cup of water with 4 green lettuce leaves, 1 small onion, 2 tablespoons of butter, sprig of parsley, ¼ teaspoon sugar, pinch of thyme, salt and pepper to taste. The peas should be tender and the liquid almost absorbed in ½ hour.

FILLETS PIQUANTE
(Le Gourmet)

1½ lbs. fish fillets
½ tsp. salt
⅛ tsp. pepper
¼ tsp. thyme
½ tsp. tarragon, ground
2 tbsps. minced onions
1 small clove of garlic,
minced
1 cup of tomato juice
½ cup coarse crumbs

Sprinkle fish with salt, pepper and thyme. Fold each fillet loosely and secure with toothpick and place in baking dish. Add tarragon, onion, and garlic to tomato juice and pour over fish. Sprinkle crumbs over all and bake at 400 degrees 8-10 minutes depending on size of fillets, until easily flaked with fork. Serves 4.

BAKED STUFFED SALMON
(New Bedford, Massachusetts)

1 large whole salmon
6 tbsps. butter
3 tbsps. minced onion
1 qt. bread or cracker crumbs
¾ tsp. salt
½ tsp. pepper
½ cup warm water
1 tsp. sage
1 tsp. Worcestershire sauce

Melt butter in skillet and sauté onion until golden. Add dry ingredients and seasonings with enough water to moisten. Lay salmon in sink and pour boiling water over sides and skin will peel off easily. Salt cavity and add stuffing. Tie with a string. Place 3-4 strips of bacon on top and bake at 400 degrees for 1 hour, or until fish flakes easily. Remove string; place on platter; garnish with fresh parsley and serve with sour cream sauce (see sauces). Serves 4-6.

DOVER HOUSE ROLL-UPS
(Moi)

4 5-oz. flounder fillets (or
sole)
4 3-oz. slices smoked salmon
½ tsp. cayenne pepper
1 tsp. salt
1 10-oz. package frozen
chopped spinach or 2 cups of
fresh
¼ cup lemon juice
¼ lb. fresh mushrooms
2 tbsps. sour cream

Sprinkle fish with cayenne and salt. Thaw and drain frozen spinach—chop and spoon in an even layer over fillets. Place salmon slice over spinach. Roll carefully and secure with toothpicks. Brush with lemon juice. Bake at 400 degrees for 10 minutes. While baking, sauté chopped mushrooms in butter and add to remainder of spinach with sour cream and spoon over roll-ups. Serves 4.

POACHED SALMON
(Ruth's)

4 salmon steaks–1" thick
1 large onion, thinly sliced
1 carrot, scraped and thinly sliced
2 cups of chicken bouillon
Salt and pepper to taste

Place salmon in well greased glass baking dish. Cover with sliced onion and carrot. Sprinkle with salt and pepper. Heat bouillon and pour around fish. Place in preheated oven at 375 degrees and bake for 20 minutes. Remove and discard vegetables and carefully place fish on platter. Serve with 2 parts sour cream mixed with mayonnaise and fresh, chopped chives or dill. Serves 4.

FILLET OF SOLE ARGENTEUIL
(Gerard Labrosse, Chef)

6 fillets of sole
6 spears of asparagus—fresh
cooked or frozen
½ cup dry white wine
4 shallots, or 1 med.
onion—chopped
1 tbsp. butter
3 tbsps. flour
1 cup heavy cream
3 egg yolks
2 tbsps. grated Swiss cheese
Salt and pepper to taste
Pinch of cayenne
1 fresh lemon

Butter a small Pyrex casserole or oven platter and place the shallots in the butter. Roll a spear of asparagus in each fillet and secure with a toothpick. Add dry wine and poach slowly in oven at 325 degrees for 10 minutes. Remove fillets and keep warm on a pretty platter and prepare the following sauce: Place 1 tablespoon of butter in a small saucepan. Add flour to make a white roux. Gradually stir in the fish stock used in poaching the fillets. Add the heavy cream, salt, pepper, and cayenne. Remove from stove. Beat 3 egg yolks—then whisk them briskly into the sauce. Strain through a sieve and return to stove heating *just* to

boiling—DO NOT BOIL.
Remove toothpicks from fish
rolls and pour sauce over them, a
squeeze of lemon juice, and
sprinkle lightly with grated
cheese. Place under broiler,
watching constantly, until lightly
browned. Serve with rice pilaf.
Serves 3-6, depending on size of
fillets.

SOLE SUPREME

4 sole fillets
1/2 lb. fresh sliced mushrooms
1/4 cup chopped parsley
1 tbsp. fresh lemon juice
1 tbsp. margarine
1/2 tsp. flour
3/4 cup heavy cream
1/2 tbsp. grated Parmesan cheese
1/2 tbsp. fine bread crumbs
Salt, paprika, white pepper to taste

Sprinkle fillets lightly with salt and pepper. Arrange in shallow baking dish—buttered. Sprinkle with parsley. In saucepan, melt margarine with lemon juice; add mushrooms, a little salt and sauté over low heat 10-12 minutes, stir occasionally. Blend in flour and gradually add cream; simmer, stirring until thick. Pour sauce over fish and sprinkle with cheese, bread crumbs, and a little paprika. Bake at 475 degrees for 20-25 minutes or until golden. Serves 4.

FILLETS DE SOLE AU VIN BLANC
(Normandy, France)

1 ½ lbs. flounder fillets
1 cup dry white wine
Salt and pepper to taste
1 finely chopped shallot
¼ lb. sliced mushrooms
2 egg yolks
½ cup heavy cream
1 tsp. chopped parsley

Spread fillets in a shallow, buttered baking dish. Add wine, sprinkle with salt, pepper, and shallot. Spread mushrooms over this. Dot with butter and bake in moderate oven for 20 minutes, or until cooked, but still firm. Drain off liquid into a small saucepan (keep fillets warm) and simmer down to one cup content. Mix egg yolks briskly with ½ cup of heavy cream and stir carefully into reduced fish stock. Add 1 teaspoon of chopped parsley and pour all over fillets. Glaze very briefly under the broiler. Serves 4.

GREEK DELIGHT
(Peas Parnassus-Dr. Andrikides)

1½ lbs. fillet of sole
½ lemon
1 tsp. butter
Salt and pepper to taste

SAUCE:
17 oz. can of peas (pour off liquid)
2 tbsps. butter
8 small whole onions cooked
1 cup stewed tomatoes
½ tsp. salt
2 tsps. cornstarch

Place fillets in buttered baking dish, sprinkle with salt and pepper and juice of lemon. Dot with butter and bake at 425 degrees for 10-15 minutes. Prepare sauce: Mix peas, onions and tomatoes and salt. Simmer 5 minutes. Mix ¼ of liquid with cornstarch and stir into sauce—spoon over fish—bake 10 minutes more and serve. Serves 4.

GINGER FISH FILLETS

1 lb. fish fillets
½ tsp. garlic salt
¼ cup tomato juice
3 tbsps. soy sauce
½ tsp. ground ginger
Lime and lemon slices for
garnish

Sprinkle fillets with garlic salt. Combine tomato juice, soy sauce, and ginger. Pour over fish. Let stand for 10 minutes. Broil 4 inches from unit. Serve with lime or lemon slices. Serves 2.

GINGER FILLETS

1 lb. fish fillets
12 oz. ginger ale
1 med. onion chopped
1 green pepper chopped
1 med. tomato chopped
1 cup sliced mushrooms
½ tsp. seasoned salt
¼ tsp. seasoned pepper
Dash of garlic

Place fillets in shallow baking dish and cover with ginger ale (1 cup). Bake at 450 degrees for 10 minutes or until you can flake fish with fork. While fish is baking, heat remaining ginger ale and sauté onion, pepper, tomato, and mushroom in butter, covered, until soft. Add to ginger ale, add salt and pepper and pour over fish. Makes 2-4 servings.

CHINESE HALIBUT STEAK

2 1-lb. halibut steaks
½ cup fresh mushrooms, sliced
2 tsps. ginger
1 ½ tsps. grated lemon rind
2 tbsps. soy sauce
2 tbsps. chicken bouillon

Place fish in baking dish. Combine mushrooms, ginger, lemon rind, soy sauce, and bouillon and pour over fish. Cover and refrigerate for 30 minutes. Steam on rack over boiling water for 20 minutes. (Make sure dish is entirely out of water.) Serves 4-6.

BLUSHING SWORDFISH

1 ½ lb. swordfish
2 tbsps. chopped pimento
2 tbsps. chopped onion
2 tbsps. butter
2 tbsps. flour
1 tsp. salt
¼ tsp. pepper
¼ tsp. Angostura Bitters (optional)

Place fish in baking pan. Mix pimento, onions, butter, flour, salt and pepper into a paste and spread on fish. Sprinkle with bitters and bake at 350 degrees, 30 minutes. Serves 6.

ELEGANT SWORDFISH
(Moi)

1 lb. swordfish steak
½ cup mayonnaise
1 tsp. parsley flakes
¼ tsp. Angostura Bitters
½ tsp. lemon juice
Salt and pepper to taste

Dry fish off well. Mix all ingredients, brush one side of steak with mixture and place under broiler, 3-4 inches from unit. Broil until bubbly and starting to brown (5-8 minutes depending on thickness of piece). Turn gently, brush mixture on other side and repeat as above. Serve with lemon wedges and fresh sprigs of parsley. Serves 2-3.

SAVOURY SWORDFISH

1 lb. swordfish
¼ cup lemon juice
½ cup tomato juice
2 tbsps. mint flakes
⅛ tsp. Angostura Bitters
(optional)

Combine lemon juice and tomato juice. Dip fish in mixture and sprinkle both sides with mint und bitters—bake at 400 degrees for 8-10 minutes depending on thickness of fish. Serves 2-3.

BAYOU PERCH

1 lb. perch fillets
1 tsp. salt
2 tbsps. finely chopped celery
2 tbsps. tomato juice
½ tsp. cayenne
2 tsps. chives

Slowly pour tomato juice over fish in baking pan. Sprinkle with salt and pepper, celery and chives. Bake at 375 degrees for 15 minutes. Serves 2.

BROILED SHAD ROE
(Jo's)

1 pair shad roe
Salt and pepper to taste
1 tbsp. of butter
2 tbsps. lemon juice
2 strips bacon

Mix melted butter and lemon juice and brush gently on roe. Sprinkle with salt and pepper. Lay strip of bacon over each side and broil for 4-5 minutes, depending on size of roe, 4 inches from unit. Serves 2.

BAKED SHAD
(Aunt Maude's)

1 5-lb. shad cleaned and split
1 tsp. salt
½ tsp. seasoned pepper
⅛ tsp. mace
½ cup onion bouillon
1 garlic bud crushed
Lemon slices for garnish

Sprinkle shad with salt and pepper and place in baking dish. Add mace and garlic to bouillon. Pour slowly over fish and bake at 400 degrees for 20 minutes or until fish flakes easily. Garnish with lemon slices.

GAUCHO GOLDEN FISH

2 8-oz. swordfish steaks
1 cup lemon juice
1 cup water
1 tbsp. allspice
Salt and pepper to taste
¼ tsp. Tabasco sauce

In a large skillet combine lemon juice, water, spice, salt, pepper, and Tabasco. Heat to simmer—*do not boil.* Add fish and simmer about $\bar{4}$ minutes on each side (6 minutes if really thick steaks). Serves 2.

MARINATED SWORDFISH

⅔ cup oil (olive preferred)
⅓ cup wine vinegar
1 lb. swordfish ½" thick
Salt and pepper to taste
Parsley and lemon wedges for
garnish

Cut swordfish into serving portions. Mix oil and vinegar, add swordfish and marinate for 3-4 hours in refrigerator. Remove from marinade; broil 12-13 minutes per side. Add salt and pepper. Garnish with parsley and lemon slices. Serves 4.

TROUT AMANDINE
(Joseph's)

Trout, cleaned and wiped
dry
3 tbsps. butter
Corn meal
Salt and pepper to taste
½ cup slivered almonds
2-3 tbsps. butter

Add salt and pepper to corn meal and roll fish in mixture, covering well. Melt butter in frying pan and sauté fish 10 minutes on one side, turn carefully with spatula and brown on other side. While fish is cooking sauté almonds in 2-3 tablespoons of butter and pour over fish when transferred to platter. Servings depend on size of fish.

BAKED RAINBOW TROUT
(Suzy's)

8 6-oz. rainbow trout, boned
8 large slices tomato
8 large mushroom caps
16 small strips of king crab
meat (optional)
Melted butter
Salt and pepper to taste
Paprika
½ tsp. dill (fresh if
available)
1 cup cashew or macadamia
nuts, chopped
Shredded lettuce (optional)
6 oz. wild rice
¼ tsp. soy sauce

Arrange trout in shallow well buttered pan. Season with salt, pepper, and paprika. Cook rice as directed on package. Drain and spoon into opening of each trout and top with slice of tomato and a mushroom. Arrange thin strips of crab on each and brush lightly with butter. Bake at 350 degrees until trout meat is white—about 20 minutes. Serve as it comes from the oven or on a bed of shredded lettuce with a sauce of nuts lightly browned in ¼ cup of butter and soy sauce. Serves 8.

SAUCY TROUT
(Louis)

4 trout filleted
2 cups seasoned breadcrumbs
1 cup barbecue sauce
1 cup brown sugar
1 cup catsup
2 tbsps. French mustard
1 med. onion minced

Dip fish in barbecue sauce; roll in bread crumbs until thoroughly covered. Bake at 325 degrees for 20 to 30 minutes until brown. Combine sugar, catsup, mustard, and onion and simmer 3-4 minutes until onion is transparent. Serve over hot fish. Garnish with lemon slices and fresh parsley. Serves 4.

SVELTE GEFILTE FISH
(Hattie's)

1 lb. whitefish
1 lb. pike
1 rib celery
2 tbsps. onion flakes
1 tsp. garlic powder (could
do with less)
2 tsps. salt
1 tsp. pepper
2 tbsps. unflavored gelatin
1 cup cold water
Radish buds or slices
Green pepper rings
Horseradish

Cut fish in small strips (be sure all bones and skin are removed); slice celery and finely grind together with fish. Add onion flakes, garlic powder, salt and pepper, and mix well. Sprinkle gelatin over mixture. Add water, 1/4 cup at a time until mixture will not absorb any more. Shape into an oval loaf. Bake on rack at 350 degrees for 1-1 1/4 hours. Garnish top of loaf with pepper rings centered with radish buds or slices. Serve with horseradish on the side. Serves 6-8.

FISH FRANCISCO

4 halibut steaks
1 cup sauterne
2 tbsps. butter
Lemon slices
1 small onion—chopped
Salt and pepper to taste
Sprigs of fresh parsley

Marinate fish steaks in sauterne and refrigerate for 3 hours. Place fish and wine in shallow baking dish. Sprinkle with salt and pepper. Bake for 25 minutes at 375 degrees. Spread with butter and chopped onion—put under broiler for 5 minutes. Pour off excess liquid and garnish with lemon slices and fresh parsley. Serves 4.

YUMMY FRIED FISH
(Missouri)

Salt
8 small pieces fresh fish
1 cup pancake flour
¾ cup milk
1 egg
¼ cup Seven-Up

Salt fish and shake in a bag of pancake flour to cover pieces well. Let set 20 minutes. Mix pancake flour with milk. Beat egg with Seven-Up, add to flour and milk mixture—should be thin. Add more Seven-Up if mixture thickens. Cover fish with batter; drop into hot fat (400 degrees). Cook 4-6 minutes. Serves 4-8.

SOLE WITH NEWBURG SAUCE
(Humarock Lodge)

4 med. fillets of sole
1 chicken lobster, cooked,
shelled, and chopped
2 tbsps. butter
2 tbsps. olive oil
Pinch of cayenne
Salt and pepper to taste
2/3 cup of sherry
1/4 cup brandy
1 1/2 cup heavy cream
1/2 cup chicken bouillon
Beurre Manie
(2 tbsps. butter & 3 tbsps.
flour mixed to paste)

In skillet poach fillets in Court Bouillon (see sauces) for 8-10 minutes. Remove to shallow baking dish and prepare Newburg sauce as follows: Heat butter, oil, bouillon, and seasoning; when mixture starts to simmer, remove from heat, add brandy and flame; add sherry and simmer gently 3-4 minutes. Add cream and lobster. Cover and simmer 10 minutes more. Thicken with Beurre Manie. Pour sauce over fillets and pop into oven for a few more minutes at 375 degrees before serving. Serves 4.

FILLETS OF SOLE BONNE FEMME
(Two Bridges, Dartmoor, England)

2 tbsps. butter
2 shallots finely chopped
1 tbsp. dried or ⅓ cup fresh chopped parsley
¼ lb. mushrooms chopped
1 4-oz. glass of white wine
Beurre Manie (see above recipe)
Lemon juice–Salt and pepper to taste
4 fillets of sole

Add shallots and ½ of mushrooms to melted butter; place fillets on top and cover with rest of mushrooms. Season to taste, add wine, and simmer for 10 minutes. Remove fish to serving dish. Reduce liquid to ½; add few drops of lemon juice and thicken with a little Beurre Manie. Pour over fillets and sprinkle with chopped parsley. Serves 4.

BAKED FISH—I

Moisten one cup of cracker or toasted bread crumbs with three tablespoons of butter; add one teaspoon each of chopped onion, pickle, salt, and pepper.

Clean and dry fish; rub with salt inside and out; stuff and sew with fine thread; cut gashes in each side; rub all over with soft butter, salt and pepper, and place narrow strips of bacon in the gashes and in bottom of pan. Sprinkle lightly with flour and put into a hot oven without water. When it begins to brown, baste with half water and half melted butter every 10 minutes. Bake for one hour. Remove thread and place fish on a hot platter. Around it pour either hollandaise sauce or drawn butter and lemon slices. Place sprigs of fresh parsley in the gashes.

BAKED FISH—II

Use any preferred fish weighing four or five pounds. Clean and sprinkle lightly with salt and pepper. Prepare a stuffing of one cup of fine bread crumbs, one tablespoon each of minced onion and parsley, ½ cup of butter, juice and grated rind of one lemon, one cup of chopped oysters—raw; salt and pepper to taste.

Fill fish with the stuffing, sew it up, just cover the bottom of the pan with hot water and lay in the fish with lumps of butter spread over it. Place in hot oven. Bake about one hour, basting frequently with drippings. After cooking for 45 minutes spread fish with a white sauce, sprinkle thickly with bread crumbs and butter, and bake until brown. Garnish with fried oysters (optional) and parsley and serve with hollandaise sauce.

SHELLFISH
ENTREES
AND
SALADS

CRAB MEAT CANAILLE
(Norma's – Hotel Vendome Memoire)

2 tbsps. butter
2 tbsps. flour
1 cup milk
¼ lb. cheddar cheese, cut up
¼ tsp. lemon pepper
¼ tsp. sea salt
2 tbsps. sherry
1 egg yolk beaten with fork
½ lb. crab meat, fresh or frozen
½ lb. sautéed fresh mushrooms

Melt butter in pan, stir in flour and milk and add cheese—stir until cheese melts, add seasonings, sherry, and egg yolk. Mix well and pour over crab meat and mushrooms placed in bottom of buttered baking dish. Top with crumbs lightly. Bake at 375 degrees for 15-20 minutes or until golden. Serve piping hot on toast points with fresh parsley garnish. Serves 4.

SHRIMP CARIBBEAN

1 cup tomato juice
1/4 tsp. Worcestershire sauce
Grated rind of 1 lime
1/4 tsp. salt
6 tbsps. lime juice
2 7-oz. cans water packed
tuna, drained
1 lb. cooked shrimp
Lime wedges for garnish

Cook tomato juice until reduced to 1/2 cup. Cool, then add Worcestershire sauce, grated lime rind, salt, and lime juice. Pour mixture over tuna fish and shrimp combined in bowl and stir well. Serve on lettuce leaves and garnish with lime slices. Serves 4.

CRAB PIERRE

1/2 lb. king crab
Cherry tomatoes, halved
2 hard cooked eggs, sliced
Stuffed olives, halved
Endive—separate leaves (may
substitute lettuce)

Cut crab meat into bite size pieces. Arrange on luncheon plates in endive leaves, with tomatoes, eggs, and olives arranged in between. Serve Pierre dressing on the side.

3/4 cup chili sauce
1/2 cup mayonnaise
1 tsp. minced chives
1/2 tsp. basil
1/2 tsp. Worcestershire sauce

Pierre Dressing

Mix ingredients.
Serves 2.

SHRIMP CREOLE
(Louisiana)

1 cup chopped onions
1½ cups chopped celery
1 large green pepper chopped
1 clove garlic minced
¼ cup butter
1 small can tomato sauce
1 cup water (add more if needed)
2 tsps. dried parsley
Salt to taste
⅛ tsp. cayenne
1 large bay leaf
1 lb. fresh cooked shrimp

Mix onion, celery, green pepper, and garlic in butter and simmer until onion is transparent and celery tender. Remove from heat and stir in tomato sauce, water, and seasonings. Simmer uncovered 10 minutes. Stir in shrimp. Heat to boiling; cover and simmer gently 10 minutes. Serve over saffron rice. Serves 6.

CRAB COQUILLE
(Canada)

1 cup dry wine
⅔ cup water
3 sprigs fresh parsley
1 small onion, chopped
1 lb. Alaska king crab
2 tbsps. butter
½ lb. fresh mushrooms
chopped
2 tbsps. flour
1 can condensed cream of
chicken soup
¾ cup heavy cream
3 tbsps. lemon juice
3 tbsps. melted butter
3 tbsps. Parmesan cheese
6 tbsps. fine dry bread
crumbs

Combine wine, water, parsley, and onion in small saucepan and heat over moderate flame until just to the boil. Add crab meat and simmer 5 minutes. Drain, reserving ¾ cup of broth. Break crab meat into bite size pieces. Melt butter in large frying pan and sauté mushrooms until lightly browned, 6-8 minutes. Blend in flour. Add soup, cream, and lemon juice and cook over low heat stirring until thickened. Stir in reserved broth and fold in crab meat. Spoon into individual pastry shells or heatproof ramekins. Mix 3 tablespoons melted butter, grated cheese and crumbs. Spoon over crab mixture. Place under broiler 3 inches from heat for 3-4 minutes or until lightly browned. Serves 8.

SIMPLE SOFT-SHELL CRABS

Remove the sandbag and spongy substance from the sides. Rinse and drop them in a pan of boiling vegetable oil until brown. Garnish with watercress and serve with drawn butter.

CRAB SHREDS

¼ cup chicken bouillon
¾ lb. cooked crab meat
1 tbsp. ginger
¼ tsp. cooking sherry
1 tsp. sugar
¼ cup soy sauce
¼ cup sliced scallions

Heat bouillon in skillet. Add crab meat and ginger and cook over low heat for 4 minutes. Add sherry, sugar, and soy sauce. Cook over low heat stirring constantly until mixture is heated thoroughly. Add scallions. Serve on a nest of boiled rice.
Serves 2-4.

CRAB GRATINE

8 oz. crab meat
2 oz. bread crumbs
4 oz. grated cheese
1/4 tsp. powdered mustard
1/2 tsp. cayenne
1/2 tsp. salt
1/4 tsp. pepper
1/2 tsp. Worcestershire sauce
3 tbsps. cream
1/2 oz. butter

Add dry ingredients to crab meat and mix well. Add Worcestershire sauce and enough cream to bind—fairly soft. Put in shells or ramekins and bake 20 minutes at 400 degrees. Serve with slices of banana or apple fried in butter until brown. Serves 4.

SHRIMP AND LOBSTER MARINADE
(Port Arthur, Providence, Rhode Island)

1/2 lb. cooked shrimp
1/2 lb. cooked lobster
1 cup of marinara sauce
2 16-oz. cans of bean sprouts
drained

Coarsely chop shrimp and lobster. Add to marinara sauce (see sauces)—cook over low heat for 5 minutes until well heated. Warm bean sprouts and drain thoroughly. Spoon shrimp and lobster over sprouts. Serves 4.

POLYNESIAN SHRIMP

1 med. pepper, sliced
1 cup orange juice
1 tbsp. soy sauce
1 lb. cooked shrimp
2 tbsps. water
2 tbsps. lemon juice
1 small can pineapple
chunks

In skillet, cook pepper in water just until tender, add juices, soy sauce, and pineapple. Cook gently until thick, stirring constantly. Add shrimp. Heat thoroughly but gently. Serves 4.

UDANG BAKAR
(Baked Shrimp–Dutch)

2 lbs. raw shrimp
½ cup butter
2 cloves minced garlic
2 tsps. salt
½ cup chopped parsley
Lemon wedges

Split shrimp with scissors and remove from shells and devein. Arrange in shallow baking dish. Sprinkle with melted butter, garlic, salt, and ½ of parsley. Broil about 4-5 inches from unit for 7 minutes on each side (less if shrimp are very small). Cook only until pink. Sprinkle with remaining parsley and serve with lemon wedges. Serves 6-8.

PEQUOSETTE LOBSTER NEWBURG

1 lb. lobster meat
6 tbsps. butter
5½ tbsps. flour
1 cup all purpose cream
2 cups milk
Pepper to taste
½ tsp. salt
¼ tsp. thyme
8 tbsps. catsup
2½ tbsps. Worcestershire sauce
6 tsps. sherry

Cut up lobster meat, blend butter, flour, cream, and milk in top of double broiler. Add catsup, Worcestershire sauce, and seasoning. Cook only long enough to blend well and heat thoroughly. Add sherry just before serving. Serves 4-6.

CARROLL CORNISH'S CRAB MEAT LORENZO

*1½ cups cooked crab
meat–flaked
½ cup mayonnaise
½ cup heavy cream, whipped
¼ cup catsup
1 tsp. Worcestershire sauce
2 tbsps. chopped chives
Paprika
3 hard-cooked eggs, sliced
6 lemon slices
Salt and pepper to taste*

Season crab meat with salt and pepper. Place on a bed of lettuce. Combine mayonnaise, whipped cream, catsup, and Worcestershire sauce. Pour mixture over crab meat and sprinkle with chives and paprika. Garnish with egg and lemon slices. Serves 6.

ELIZABETHAN LOBSTER PIE
(Gore Hotel, England)

2 1½ -2 lb. lobsters
3 tsps. vinegar
½ lb. butter or margarine melted
1 cup of bread crumbs dried
Salt and pepper to taste
1 large bay leaf

Boil lobsters and remove all meat. Cut each tail in four pieces and lay in bottom of baking dish. Chop all remaining meat and mix with vinegar, butter, and crumbs with seasoning, and tamale (the green part of the lobster); cover tails with this and then cover all with your favorite pie crust. Bake in oven at 325 degrees for ½ hour or until pie crust golden brown. Serves 4-6.

LOBSTER MOUSSE
(Major's)

2 envelopes unflavored
gelatin (2 tbsps.)
¼ cup cold water
1 cup boiling water
1 cup boiling chicken broth
4 cups lobster meat, cut up
small
1 cup mayonnaise
1 tsp. salt
¼ cup chopped pimento
1 cup whipped cream
Lettuce
Sliced tomatoes

Soften gelatin in cold water. Dissolve in boiling water and chicken broth. Cool until slightly thickened. Fold in lobster, mayonnaise, salt, and pimento. Fold in whipped cream last. Pour mixture into mold and chill. Unmold on a platter bedded with lettuce. Garnish edges with sliced tomatoes; serve with sour cream dressing. Serves 8.

BAKED STUFFED LOBSTER
(Fritz)

12 crushed saltines
1 can minced clams
2 tbsps. Worcestershire sauce
½ tsp. celery salt
¼ tsp. black pepper
¼ cup melted butter or
margarine
1 clam can of milk
Grated cheese
Paprika
4 1½ -2 lb. fresh lobsters

Mix saltines, clams, seasoning, melted butter, and milk. If a little dry add more milk. Place live lobster on its back on a board; hold firmly with left hand between claws and tail. Cut body from head to tip of tail and split open. Fill lobster with mixture, place in broiler pan and sprinkle with cheese and paprika. Dot with small cubes of butter. Place a little water in bottom of pan. Bake at 450 degrees for 20 minutes. If tails curl up, remove from oven and turn down and put back in oven.

HOMARD À LA CRÈME
(Lobster in Cream)

Slice the meat of a 2 lb. boiled lobster and heat pieces in 2 table-spoons of hot butter for 1 or 2 minutes. Add salt and pepper to taste, and a little paprika. Pour on 1 tablespoon warmed brandy, ignite and shake pan back and forth gently until flames die. Beat 2 egg yolks with ¾ cup cream and add 2 tablespoons of sherry. Pour over lobster and simmer gently, stirring constantly until thickened. DO NOT BOIL. Serve over toast points in individual warmed casseroles garnished with fresh parsley. Serves 2-4.

OYSTERS IMPERIAL
(Bill's)

To liquor from one pint of oysters add a pinch of salt and paprika, a half cup each of minced celery and cooked mushrooms, two table-spoons of butter blended with one of flour and six of cream, stirring constantly; add the oysters, and when the edges curl add two egg yolks beaten, and a third of a cup each of cream and sherry. Serve on toast. Serves 4.

MINCED OYSTERS
(Tennessee)

Wash and chop two pints of oysters. Add one cup of browned crumbs, two hard-boiled egg yolks, two raw yolks, two tablespoons of butter, one each of minced parsley, lemon juice, and tomato catsup, a dash of nutmeg, salt and pepper to taste. Simmer 10 minutes. Add two tablespoons of thick cream. Put into buttered shells or ramekins, top lightly with crumbs and bits of butter. Place shells in a pan and brown quickly in a hot oven 400 degrees 10-15 minutes. Serves 2-4.

OYSTER SPREE
(Tim's)

1 qt. fresh shucked oysters
1 tsp. salt
½ tsp. cayenne pepper
¾ cup bread crumbs
¾ cup milk
1 tbsp. cooking sherry

Parboil oysters in simmering water for 3 minutes. Place in shallow baking dish. Sprinkle with salt and pepper, cover with crumbs. Combine milk and sherry and pour over all. Broil about 3 minutes, 3 inches from unit. Serves 4-5.

SCALLOPED OYSTERS AND CORN
(Camille's)

1 pt. oysters (reserve liquid)
¼ cup butter or margarine
2 cups coarsely crumbled
crackers
1 12-oz. can of whole kernel
corn–drained
Salt and pepper to taste
6 tbsps. cream

Melt butter and add crumbs. Mix well. Butter a 12x8x2 casserole and spread 1 oz. of crumbs over the bottom. Arrange half of drained oysters and half of corn over these—season lightly. Scatter ½ of remaining crumbs over this, add remaining oysters and corn—again season lightly. Mix ¾ cup of oyster liquid with 6 tablespoons of cream and drizzle over all. Chill. About 30 minutes before dinner, heat oven to 425 degrees. Top oyster mixture with remaining crumbs and bake about 20 minutes or until crumbs are browned. Serves 6.

MORRIS' OYSTERS
(Sir William Osler's butler)

3 pts. oysters
5 hard-boiled eggs
¼ lb. butter
1 pt. heavy cream
2 heaping tbsp. flour
1 gill of sherry

Cook oysters gently in a flat pan over moderate heat about 10 minutes until edges are ruffled; drain. Mash the yolks of the hard-boiled eggs very fine, add butter and flour; rub to a smooth paste. Heat the cream quite hot and add slowly to paste stirring constantly. Put mixture in a saucepan and let cook slowly until it thickens, stirring constantly. If it gets too thick add more cream. Add oysters and cook 5 minutes longer. Pour in sherry 2 or 3 minutes before serving. Season with red and black pepper to taste. Serve in a soup plate on toasted split English muffins with a slice of ham. Serves 8.

OYSTER BARBECUE
(Sully's)

2 lbs. oysters (fresh and
shucked)
1 tsp. salt
½ tsp. pepper
¼ cup minced onions
2 tbsps. chopped chives
2 tbsps. chopped celery leaves
¼ cup chicken bouillon
1 tbsp. lemon juice
10" squares of heavy duty
foil

Sprinkle oysters with salt and pepper. Divide oysters into equal portions on 10 inch squares of foil. Sprinkle each portion with onion, chives, and celery leaves. Combine bouillon and lemon juice—pour over each portion equally. Bring edges of foil together securely so that no juice escapes. Place on red hot coals—or bake at 400 degrees for 12 minutes. Serves 6-8.

CORNY OYSTERS
(Moi)

1 pt. of plump oysters
¾ cup of milk
1 egg slightly beaten
1 can of cream style corn
2 tbsps. minced onion
¼ cup minced green pepper
¼ tsp. salt
Pepper to taste
1½ cups cracker crumbs
4 tbsps. melted butter

Grease 1½ qt. baking dish. Drain oysters, but reserve liquid. Combine milk, oyster liquid, and egg. Alternate layers of corn, onion, pepper, seasoning, oysters, egg mixture, and cracker crumbs in that order. Reserve ½ cup cracker crumbs and mix with butter for topping. Bake at 350 degrees for ¼ to 1 hour until top is golden. Serves 6.

CREAMED OYSTERS
(Tennessee)

In hot sautoir (or a very heavy copper bottom saucepan) blend two tablespoons of butter with one of flour; stir and add the strained liquor from one pint of oysters. When hot add one cup of cream; when mixture thickens, add the oysters. Serve with croutons.

OYSTERS FITZPATRICK

*1 pt. of oysters, partially
drained
1 pinch of oregano
1 clove of garlic (whole, and
remove before serving)
2 tbsps. minced onion
½ cup bread crumbs
½ cup tomato sauce*

Spread oysters in small casserole dish with a little of their liquid. Pour on tomato sauce, sprinkle with oregano, onion and top with crumbs. Add garlic in middle of top. Bake at 375 degrees about 15 minutes until top crisps. Serves 4.

FRIED OYSTERS
(Camille's)

Select large plump oysters. Dry in folds of soft cloth. Sprinkle with salt and pepper, roll in fine bread crumbs, dip in beaten egg, then again in crumbs. (Corn meal may be substituted for crumbs.) Have hot cooking oil 4 inches deep in frying pan (use a basket if you have one), put a single layer of oysters into the fat. Cook one and a half minutes. Drain and serve at once. Two dozen oysters require two eggs diluted with one tablespoon of milk, one teaspoon of salt, $\frac{1}{2}$ teaspoon of pepper and 3 cups of crumbs.

TARTARE OYSTERS
(Baltimore)

Scald oysters in their liquor until plump and edges are curled. Chill, then cut them in halves lengthwise. Line oyster shells with curled lettuce. Place oysters, pyramid shape, in each. Cover with tartar sauce.

HEYDAY SCALLOPED OYSTERS

3 1/2 cups coarse crumbled
saltines
2 pts. of oysters (drain and
save liquid)
3 1/2 cups liquid (oyster
liquid and milk combined)
1 1/2 tsps. pepper
1/2 tsp. cayenne pepper
1/2 cup butter or margarine

Butter a 2 1/2 quart casserole and cover bottom with 3/4 cup of crumbs, place 1/2 of oysters over crumbs; sprinkle with pepper and dot with butter. Repeat layers, ending with crumbs and butter. Pour liquid over all. Bake 1 hour at 375 degrees or until top is crusty. Serves 8.

OYSTERS ROCKEFELLER
(Hotel Touraine, Boston)

36 oysters in shell
2 cups of cooked spinach
4 tbsps. chopped onion
2 bay leaves crushed
1 tbsp. parsley chopped
1/2 tsp. celery salt
1/2 tsp. salt
6 drops Tabasco sauce
1/2 cup bread crumbs
6 tbsps. butter

Shuck and drain oysters and place them on deep half of oyster shell. Chop up (or put through grinder) spinach, onion, bay leaves, and parsley. Add seasonings and sauté in butter 5 minutes. Add bread crumbs and mix well. Spread over oysters and bake at 400 degrees for 10 minutes. Garnish with thin lemon slices. Serves 6.

BANTRY BAY SCALLOPS
(Colonial Club)

2 tbsps. butter or margarine
1 tbsp. brandy–warmed
1 tbsp. lemon juice
½ tsp. salt
⅛ tsp. pepper
¼ cup light cream
Dash of cayenne pepper
1 pt. of scallops (bay scallops
if available–if deep sea cut
up smaller)

Sauté scallops in butter for 3 minutes. Add brandy, ignite. Sprinkle with lemon juice, salt, pepper, and cayenne. Add cream—heat gently, DO NOT BOIL. Serve in small, individual, warmed, casseroles with toast points. Serves 4.

MYSTIC SCALLOPS
(Canadian)

3 tbsps. butter
½ tsp. minced onion
½ tsp. parsley flakes
⅛ tsp. tarragon leaves
¹/₁₆ tsp. garlic salt
¹/₁₆ tsp. black pepper
1 tsp. lemon juice
1 tsp. salt
1 pt. bay scallops
½ cup soft bread crumbs

Soften butter and add onion, parsley flakes, tarragon, garlic, salt, pepper, and lemon juice. Arrange scallops in 8 shells, or small individual casseroles. Top each with 1 teaspoon of herbed mixture. Bake in a very hot oven, 500 degrees, for 5 minutes. Serves 8.

COQUILLE ST. JACQUES
(Au Beauchamp, Boston)

1 tbsp. oil
2 lbs. deep sea scallops
2 tbsps. shallots or green
onion
½ tsp. garlic, chopped
1 cup tomato puree,
concentrated
1 tbsp. brandy
2 cups white wine
1 cup fish stock or clam juice
3 bay leaves, pinch of thyme,
parsley, salt, pepper, cayenne
(easy does it)
1 tbsp. cornstarch

Sauté scallops in oil, not too golden. Add shallots and garlic. Cook approximately 3-4 minutes. Add other ingredients—cook approximately 7 more minutes over medium heat. Serves 4-6.

COQUILLES SAINT-JACQUES
(Also Superb!)

¾ pt. sea scallops
2 tbsps. butter
1 chopped shallot (or small white onion)
2 tbsps. fine bread crumbs
¾ cup white wine
1 tsp. finely chopped parsley
½ tsp. salt and pepper to taste
Parmesan cheese

Cut scallops into small pieces. Sauté gently 3 minutes in butter, a little pepper, and shallot. Add bread crumbs and wine; sauté 8-10 minutes or until sauce is slightly reduced. Add parsley and salt—fill 4 scallop shells with mixture. Sprinkle with bread crumbs and cheese, dot with butter and brown lightly under broiler. Serves 4.

BRITTANY SCALLOPS

⅓ cup butter or margarine
2 tsps. chopped parsley
½ clove garlic crushed
⅔ cup bread crumbs
1 lb. bay scallops (or cut up
sea scallops)
Lemon wedges
Lemon juice

Butter six large shells or ramekins lightly. Combine butter, parsley, and garlic and stir in crumbs. Spread small amount of crumbs in center of each shell and fill with scallops to just within edge of shell. Put remaining crumbs over scallops and add just a few drops of lemon juice to each. Preheat oven to 325 degrees and bake 25-30 minutes to golden brown. DO NOT OVERCOOK. Serve hot with lemon wedges. Serves 6.

Can be wrapped in foil when cool and put in freezer to be reheated in foil when wanted.

ALLA SCAMPI SCALLOPS

½ cup chicken bouillon
1 tbsp. instant minced onion
flakes
1 large clove garlic, minced
½ tsp. Worcestershire sauce
2 tbsps. parsley flakes
⅛ tsp. oregano leaves
1 pound scallops

Simmer bouillon and seasonings for 10 minutes. Pour over scallops in baking pan; cover. Bake at 350 degrees for 8-10 minutes. Transfer pan to broiler. Broil about 3 inches from unit for 2-3 minutes or until lightly browned. Serves 2.

SHRIMP RUMAKI
(Don's)

Split cooked shrimp in half lengthwise; marinate in equal parts of soy sauce and sherry 3-4 hours. Drain and wrap each shrimp in ½ slice of bacon with thin slice of water chestnut. Place in oven at 400 degrees until bacon is crisp, 8-10 minutes. Bake on rack so fat will drain. May be broiled. Watch constantly so as not to overcook.

CHINESE SHRIMP

1 med. sized green pepper
1 cup chopped onion
2 4-oz. cans sliced
mushrooms (save liquid)
1 4-oz. can pimentos (save
liquid)
2 tbsps. butter
1 10-oz. can cashew nuts
chopped
2 5-oz. cans water chestnuts,
sliced and drained
1½ lbs. fresh, cooked shrimp
2 10½-oz. cans cream of
celery soup
3 3-oz. cans Chinese noodles

Combine pepper, onion, and simmer in mushroom and pimento juice, covered, until onion is soft. Drain. Lightly brown mushrooms in butter and combine with first mix, adding pimentos, nuts, chestnuts, and shrimp. Mix with undiluted soup and season to taste. Layer bottom of large, greased baking dish with ½ noodles, cover with shrimp mix and remaining noodles and bake at 350 degrees for 30 minutes. Serves 10.

CHINESE SHRIMP WITH LOBSTER SAUCE

1 lb. ground lean beef
1 egg, beaten
1 tbsp. sugar
1 garlic clove, crushed
2 beef bouillon cubes
1 cup hot water
*2 tbsps. cornstarch dissolved
in ¼ cup water*
1 tbsp. soy sauce
*1½ tbsps. Chinese brown
sauce (also called bead
molasses)*
½ lb. cooked shrimp

Sauté beef in skillet, breaking it up fine. If not lean, drain off excess fat. Add beaten egg, garlic, and sugar and mix well. Dissolve cubes in warm water. Mix cornstarch in ¼ cup of water and soy sauce and pour over hamburger. Mix and add brown sauce, then add shrimp. Simmer gently, stirring occasionally for 10-15 minutes. If mixture is too thick thin with a little water. Serves 4-6.

SHRIMP RAMEKINS

¼ *lb. butter*
1 ½ *lbs. uncooked shrimp,*
peeled and cleaned
½ *lb. sliced mushrooms*
¼ *lb. cream cheese*
1 *cup sour cream*
2 *tsps. salt*
¼ *tsp. pepper*
½ *tsp. paprika*
2 *tsps. chopped parsley*
¼ *cup grated Parmesan*
cheese

Melt butter in skillet, add shrimp; sauté 2 minutes, then add mushrooms. Cook 6 minutes stirring frequently. Beat cream cheese until light, place in skillet. Gradually add sour cream. Bring to boiling point. Add salt, pepper, paprika, and parsley. Mix well. Divide among six buttered ramekins or oven-proof shells. Sprinkle with Parmesan cheese. Place under broiler until delicately browned. Makes 6 servings.

BEER BATTER SHRIMP WITH FRUIT SAUCE

16 very large or 24 med.
shrimp–cooked
Juice of 1 lemon
1 cup flour
1 can beer
Another cup flour–sifted
1 tbsp. salt
1 tbsp. paprika

Sprinkle cooked shrimp with lemon juice; combine beer, sifted flour, salt and paprika stirring with a wire whisk (this is your batter), dip shrimp in flour and then into batter, allowing excess batter to drain off, deep fry until golden brown—about 5 minutes at 375 degrees. Drain on paper towel and serve immediately garnished with parsley and lemon wedges.

Fruit Sauce

¾ cup orange marmalade
4 tbsps. lemon juice
2 tbsps. orange juice
1 tbsp. prepared horseradish
½ tsp. powdered ginger
Pinch of salt
½ tsp. English mustard

Place all ingredients in blender for 15 seconds or beat 1 minute at high speed. (Also excellent dip for raw vegetables.)

SHRIMP TEMPURA
(Japan)

1 ½ lbs. fresh shrimp
1 egg
1 ⅛ cups sifted flour
1 cup of water
1 tsp. salt
Fat for frying

Shell and devein shrimp, leaving tail fins attached. Slit the undersection to prevent curling when fried. Rinse and dry thoroughly. Combine egg and water; beat slightly. Add flour and salt; beat until smooth. Dip shrimp one at a time into the batter. Fry in 2 inches of hot fat until batter is golden brown. Drain on absorbent paper toweling. Serve hot accompanied by individual bowls of Dipping Sauce. Serves 4.

DIPPING SAUCE: Combine ½ cup chicken stock or broth, 3 tablespoons soy sauce and 1 tablespoon sugar. Put 3 tablespoons into each individual bowl. Divide one tablespoon grated horseradish among the 4 bowls; mix well. Serves 4.

Note: Vegetables and fish may also be used for tempura: Use small cuts of eggplant, carrot, onion, leek, sweet or white potato, asparagus tips, whole green beans. Use small whole fish and finger-length fillets, oysters or scallops.

CREOLE SHRIMP OR CRAB

Blend two tablespoons each of butter and flour in a hot sautoir, add one tablespoon each of minced onion, green pepper, and parsley. When soft, pour in a can of tomato paste and one pound of shredded cooked crab or split cooked shrimp. Add salt and cayenne to taste and 1 teaspoon of chili powder. Simmer gently ½ hour. Serve with steamed rice.

SHRIMP CREOLE
(Moi)

3 strips of bacon
2 med. onions, sliced
1 green pepper, cut in rings
½ cup diced celery
1 #2½ can tomatoes
1 tsp. salt
1 cup cooked green peas
1 tsp. chili powder
¾ lb. cooked shrimp
3 cups hot boiled rice

Crisp bacon and remove from pan and break into ¼ inch pieces. Sauté onions in bacon drippings—add green pepper, celery, tomatoes, and salt. Cook gently about 15 minutes until sauce starts to thicken. Add peas, shrimp, and chili powder and cook 5 minutes longer. Add cooked bacon.

Pack rice into a greased 9 inch tube pan. Carefully turn out on serving platter. Pour creole in center and around ring. Serves 6.

HUFF AND PUFF SHRIMP
(Hors d'oeuvre)

2 tbsps. unflavored gelatin
3½ cups tomato juice
2 tbsps. Worcestershire sauce
2 tsps. Tabasco sauce
2 tbsps. lime juice
2 lbs. cooked shrimp

Sprinkle gelatin over tomato juice to soften. Cook over low heat stirring constantly until gelatin is dissolved. Let stand 10 minutes, stir in Worcestershire and Tabasco sauce and lime juice. Chill in refrigerator until syrupy. Place shrimp on a rack. Brush tomato mixture over shrimp and chill until glazed. Turn over gently and brush other side and chill until set. Repeat this procedure two or three times until shrimp is well coated. Serve on bed of lettuce over cracked ice.

BAKED STUFFED SHRIMP
(New Orleans)

24 large cleaned shrimp,
split part way through
1 med. onion minced
1 med. size green pepper
minced
2 tbsps. butter
¼ lb. of flaked crab meat
1 tsp. sherry
1 tsp. dry mustard
1 tsp. Worcestershire
½ tsp. salt
2 tsps. mayonnaise
1 cup medium white sauce
Grated cheddar cheese
Paprika
2 tbsps. fine bread crumbs

Cook onion and green pepper in butter until soft. Add crab meat, sherry, mustard and Worcestershire, salt, mayonnaise, white sauce, and crumbs. Stuff shrimp with mixture. Dot with butter and sprinkle lightly with cheese and paprika. Bake at 350 degrees for 10 to 15 minutes or until shrimp is pink and stuffing begins to brown.

SHRIMP MOLD
(Nora's)

1 can tomato soup, condensed
¾ cup mayonnaise
1 8-oz. pkg. cream cheese
2 pkgs. plain gelatin
½ cup onion
¾ cup celery
1 tbsp. Worcestershire sauce
½ lb. fresh cooked shrimp,
chopped

Heat soup to boiling (no water).
Add cheese and Worcestershire
sauce and stir until cheese is
dissolved. Add mayonnaise,
celery, onion, and shrimp.
Dissolve gelatin in ½ cup of
warm water. Add to above
mixture, mix well. Pour into 5
cup mold which has been greased
with mayonnaise. Put in
refrigerator to set and do not
turn out until ready to serve.
Serves 6-8.

BAKED STUFFED SHRIMP FRANCO

1 lb. fresh shrimp
¼ cup minced celery
1 tsp. minced garlic
½ cup clam juice
2 slices of cracked wheat bread
1 tsp. salt
1 tbsp. minced onion
1 tsp. Worcestershire sauce
2 tbsps. melted butter
Parsley sprigs for garnish

Cook celery and garlic in clam juice (½ of above quantity) for about 5 minutes. Drain. Combine with bread cut up in small pieces, add salt and toss lightly. Add onion, Worcestershire, butter, and remainder of clam juice. With a small sharp knife split shrimp, but do not cut through. Fan out flat and cover top with above mixture. Bake at 350 degrees for 10 minutes or until shrimp is pink. Serves 4.

SHRIMP SUPREME
(Moi)

8 jumbo shrimp (fresh)
1 pkg. frozen asparagus tips,
unthawed
1 can mushroom soup,
condensed
1 tsp. Angostura Bitters
(optional)
1 small onion chopped

Cook shrimp in salted water adding a little garlic salt—just a pinch, and a couple of peppercorns. Shuck and split shrimp and place flat side down in bottom of shallow baking dish which has been buttered. Sprinkle Angostura Bitters over top. Cover with mushroom soup and chopped onion—place asparagus spears across top, cover and bake ½ hour at 350 degrees or until bubbly. Serves 4.

Added touch: When mixture starts to bubble, sprinkle seasoned crumbs over top, raise temperature to 375 degrees, return to oven until crumbs are golden—or place under broiler 2-3 minutes until crumbs are browned.

COQUILLES ST. CATHERINE

8 oz. poached sole or cod
8 oz. cooked shrimp
2 tbsps. minced onion
¼ cup buttermilk
1 tsp. melted butter
1 tsp. paprika
Parsley for garnish

Flake fish, slice shrimp thinly (reserve 8-10 slices for garnish). Mix fish with shrimp. Combine onion and buttermilk and let stand 5 minutes. Add to fish mixture. Spoon ¼ of total mixture on 4 large scallop shells, buttered. Sprinkle with paprika. Arrange shrimp slices on each and bake at 425 degrees for 5 minutes. Garnish with parsley. Serves 4.

SHRIMP PRINCESS

1 lb. cooked shrimp
1 med. head lettuce, shredded
1/4 lb. fresh mushrooms
2 cups buttermilk
1/4 cup prepared mustard
1/8 tsp. ground sage
2 tbsps. melted butter

Remove stems from mushrooms and save to use another time. In saucepan, gradually stir buttermilk, a few drops at a time into mustard. Add sage, butter, and mushroom caps; cook over moderate heat for 10 minutes. Add shrimp, cook 5 minutes longer. Blanch lettuce by pouring boiling water over it quickly in a colander. Spread it on a platter or plates and spoon shrimp over it. Serves 4.

SHRIMP QUICKIE

2 tbsps. cooking oil
½ tsp. garlic salt
¼ tsp. ginger
1 lb. of cooked shrimp
⅓ cup of water + 1 tbsp.
⅓ cup hot catsup
1½ tsps. cornstarch
½ tsp. lemon salt
Dash of Worcestershire

Heat oil until it pings; add garlic, salt, ginger and shrimp. Cook for 3 minutes turning shrimp to heat on both sides. Add ⅓ cup of water, catsup, lemon salt, and Worcestershire and cook gently, covered, for 5 minutes. Combine cornstarch and remaining water. Add to shrimp. Cook for 5 minutes stirring constantly until the sauce thickens. Serve on a bed of hot rice to which chopped parsley has been added. Serves 4.

SHRIMP JAMBALAYA
(Camille's)

¼ lb. bacon finely cut
1 med. onion chopped
1 green pepper chopped
¼ tsp. garlic salt or powder
1 lb. cooked shrimp
1 #2 can of tomatoes
¼ tsp. Tabasco sauce
1 tsp. paprika
½ tsp. salt
1 cup uncooked rice

Crisp bacon in heavy skillet. Add onion, green pepper, and garlic, cook slowly until onion is yellow. Cook shrimp and drain off and reserve 1½ cups of water. Add tomatoes, Tabasco, paprika and salt, simmer 5 minutes and add contents of skillet. Sprinkle rice over surface, cover tightly and cook gently about 15-20 minutes. Add shrimp and cook covered 5-10 minutes longer. Serves 6-8.

POACHED SHRIMP

1 ½ lbs. fresh shrimp
2 cups water
1 tsp. salt
¼ tsp. thyme

Remove legs, but leave shells intact. Bring water to boil. Add salt and thyme, then shrimp. Simmer uncovered until shrimp turn pink (approximately 4-5 minutes). Drain—shuck and serve with dip sauce (see sauces). Serves 4.

KIPPY'S SHRIMP JOHANNA

12 oz. cooked shrimp
2 med. onions sliced
1 6-oz. can of mushrooms drained (reserve liquid)
¼ cup water
½ cup tomato juice
1 tbsp. melted butter
½ cup canned peas
Parsley sprigs for garnish

Cook onions in melted butter, covered, until soft. Add mushrooms, cook until browned. Add mushroom liquid, water and shrimp, simmer gently 5 minutes. Add peas and tomato juice, and simmer 5 minutes longer. Serve with saffron rice* and garnish with parsley sprigs. Serves 4-6.

---

*Cook rice as indicated on package. When adding butter add pinches of saffron, a tiny bit at a time, mixing after each addition until rice is a light yellow hue.

SHRIMP ORIENTAL

1/4 cup salad oil
2 large onions, sliced thin
3 cups sliced celery
2 3/4-oz. cans sliced
mushrooms
1 bag of fresh spinach,
washed and large stems
chopped
1 lb. fresh cooked shrimp
1 can water chestnuts,
drained
1 11-oz. can mandarin
orange sections, drained
2 tbsps. soy sauce
2 tbsps. sugar
2 tsps. salt

Get all ingredients ready, then layer them into a kettle and steam quickly. Pour salad oil into a 4 quart kettle, layer onions, celery, mushrooms, spinach, water chestnuts, shrimp, and orange sections. Sprinkle with soy sauce, sugar, and salt, and cover. Heat until mixture begins to steam, lower heat and simmer 10-15 minutes. Spoon into individual bowls topped with a cone of hot fluffy rice. Serves 6.

CHOWDERS
BISQUES
SOUPS
AND STEWS

BULL ROCK FISH CHOWDER

1 lb. boneless cod, haddock or
quahogs
½ cup dry white wine
2-3 tbsps. butter
3 cans cream of potato soup
1 soup can light cream
1 soup can milk
Salt and pepper to taste

Place fish in shallow baking pan
with wine and dot with butter.
Bake uncovered at 400 degrees
until fish flakes—about 15
minutes. Flake fish into mixture
of soup, cream, milk, and juices
from baking pan. Season to taste
and serve piping hot. Serves 6-8.

FISH SOUP
(Narragansett, Rhode Island)

½ lb. fillet of sole
2 tbsps. soy sauce
2 tbsps. lemon juice
2 cups clam juice
½ cup diced celery
½ cup diced carrots
6 cups chicken bouillon

Cut fish in narrow slices. Mix soy
sauce and lemon juice; pour over
fish. Refrigerate for 1 hour. In
lightly greased skillet bring clam
juice to a boil; add fish and
vegetables. Simmer 5 minutes,
drain. In saucepan bring bouillon
to a boil, add fish and
vegetables—cook over low heat
for 5 minutes. Makes 4 cups.

COCKLE SOUP
(Dublin, Ireland)

4 doz. cockles
2 heaped tbsps. butter
2 heaped tbsps. flour
2 pts. (4 cups) cockle stock
1 pt. milk
2 tbsps. chopped parsley
½ cup chopped celery
½ cup light cream
Salt and pepper to taste

Small clams, mussels or scallops can be used for this recipe—or a mixture of all four. Scrub cockles well to get rid of sand and grit. Then put them in a large saucepan, with seawater, if possible, to cover. Bring to boil when they open. Melt butter in saucepan, stir in flour, then add the strained cockle juice and milk, stirring constantly until smoothly blended. Add chopped parsley, celery, and seasoning and cook for 10 minutes. Finally add cockles, heat and serve with a little cream in each portion.

NEW BEDFORD SCALLOP STEW
(Portuguese)

6 *slices of bacon*
3 *medium onions–sliced*
1 *green pepper–cut in strips*
1 *large carrot–shaved*
1 *can #1 tomatoes–do not drain*
7 *oz. of clam juice (fresh or bottled)*
1 *tbsp. chopped parsley*
2 *tsps. of salt*
1 *large bay leaf*
1 1/2 *tsps. Worcestershire sauce*
1/4 *tsp. garlic salt or powder*
3/4 *tsp. thyme leaves crushed*
2 *large, or 3 med. potatoes–diced*
2 *stalks of celery–diced*
1 1/2 *cups of water*
1 1/2 *lbs. sea scallops–cut very large ones in two*

Crisp bacon and remove from pan, add onion, pepper, carrot, and celery to drippings, cook over low heat, stirring for 10 minutes. Add parsley, tomatoes, clam juice, salt, bay leaf, Worcestershire sauce, thyme, and 1 1/2 cups of water. Bring to a boil, reduce heat, cover and simmer 15 minutes. Add potatoes and simmer 20 minutes or until potatoes are done to fork test. Add scallops and crumble bacon on top—simmer uncovered for 15 minutes. Serve piping hot. Can be frozen. Improves with standing. Serve with tossed green salad and crusty bread. Serves 6-8.

SCALLOP BROTH
(Maine)

1 lb. of scallops
4 tbsps. butter
1 quart milk
½ cup light cream and ¼
cup heavy cream
1 tbsp. chopped chives or
parsley
Pimento
Salt and pepper to taste

If sea scallops are used, cut up small and sauté for 10 minutes in butter. Add warmed milk, salt and pepper, and heat JUST to boiling, add chives or parsley, cover and let stand for 15-20 minutes. Reheat and add cream and one or two small strips of pimento. Serve in heated bowls with a puff of salted whipped cream on top. Serves 6-8.

OYSTER STEW
(Tennessee Hunt Breakfast)

To the liquor of 4 dozen oysters add one pint of boiling water and one pint of milk, one cup of cracker crumbs, two tablespoons of butter, salt and pepper to taste. When hot—DO NOT BOIL—add oysters. Cook gently until gills ruffle. Do not augment recipe. Repeat as given as servings are requested. Cooking time is very short. Serves 10-15.

NICK PETTER'S OYSTER STEW

Place two pats of butter in a saucepan. Add a few shakes of paprika and celery salt, ½ teaspoon of Worcestershire sauce and 2 table-spoons of clam juice. Bring to bubbling, stirring constantly. Slide in 8 plump oysters. Cook about 1½ minutes, until edges curl. Add ½ pint whole milk and keep stirring until stew begins to simmer. DO NOT LET BOIL. Pour at once into man size heated bowls with a pat of butter in the bottom, another pat on top, and dust with paprika. Serve with oyster crackers. Serves 2.

PERFECT OYSTER STEW
(Grand Central Station)

Combine 2 tablespoons of flour, 1½ teaspoons of salt, ⅛ teaspoon of pepper and 2 tablespoons of water. Blend to a smooth paste. Add paste to one pint of oysters and liquid. Simmer over very low heat until edges curl; then pour into one quart of scalded milk. Remove from heat. Drop large pieces of butter on top, sprinkle with paprika and let stand 10 minutes with the lid on the pan. Serves 2-4.

MY LOBSTER STEW

3 chicken lobsters, boiled and
shelled
(Save fat, roe, tamale and
liquid in shells)
1 qt. milk
1 pt. light cream
1 tbsp. butter
Salt and pepper to taste
1 tsp. parsley flakes
½ tsp. basil
1 tsp. onion salt
4 tbsps. instant mashed
potatoes
Dash Angostura Bitters

Simmer cut up lobster meat with seasonings in butter and their own liquid for 5-10 minutes gently. Add 1 pint of milk and let cool covered (or refrigerate overnight for use following day). Reheat, DO NOT BOIL. Add balance of milk, cream, and instant potatoes, stir gently and constantly until slightly thickened. Just before serving stir in dash only of Bitters.
Serves 4-6.

MY POTATO SHRIMP SOUP

4 med. sized potatoes
3 tbsps. butter
1 tbsp. flour
1 cup milk
1 cup of potato water
½ tsp. salt
Dash of pepper
Dash of paprika
1 cup cut up shrimp
2 tbsps. chopped parsley
1 tbsp. chopped chives

Peel and cook potatoes. Drain and put through sieve or ricer. Save 1 cup of water. Melt butter, add flour and stir until smooth, add milk and simmer, stir until thickened. Add potato, water, and seasonings—simmer 5 minutes. Add shrimp and bring JUST to a boil. Remove from heat. Garnish with parsley or chives, or little of both. Serves 6.

LOW CALORIE LOBSTER STEW

1 lb. cooked lobster meat
¼ lb. diet margarine
Sherry to taste
½ pt. cream–light
1 qt. skimmed milk
2 tsps. paprika

Sauté lobster meat in margarine, add sherry and some lobster water, add cream slowly and simmer until hot, then add milk a little at a time. DO NOT BOIL. Heat just to boiling and serve. Serves 4.

ANN BROWN'S FISH CHOWDER
(Bow Lake, New Hampshire)

2½ lbs. haddock fillets
1 med. onion sliced
6 med. potatoes cubed
2 tbsps. butter or margarine
1 qt. whole milk
1 cup light cream
6 tbsps. butter or margarine
1 tbsp. salt
⅛ tsp. pepper
¼ tsp. parsley flakes
¼ tsp. thyme

Cover fillets with cold water and boil gently for about 10 minutes. Drain and save liquid. Boil cubed potatoes in fish liquid for 10 minutes or until soft. Fry onion in 2 tablespoons of butter until transparent. Scald milk and cream together. DO NOT BOIL. Add fish, potatoes, 6 tablespoons of butter, onion, seasonings, and herbs. Add 3 cups of the liquid the fish and potatoes were cooked in. Set aside to cool. Flavor improves with standing. Reheat gently to piping hot. Cover while cooling. Serves 8-10.

QUAHOG CHOWDER
(Moi)

12 large quahogs (steam open
and save liquid)
2 large potatoes, diced
1 large onion, sliced
⅛ lb. salt pork, diced
1 tsp. sugar
Pepper to taste
1 tsp. basil
1 qt. milk
1 pt. light cream

Optional: 2 tbsps. flour and ½ cup water, blend and add before milk to thicken slightly.

After steaming quahogs open, chill before chopping up. Fry out salt pork until golden brown and remove. Sauté onion in drippings until transparent. Add enough water to quahog liquid to cover potatoes and cook until soft. Add pork scraps, onions, and quahogs. Considered as chowder "guts," this can be put away or frozen for later use, or proceed as follows: Add optional thickening if desired, then milk and cream. Let cool and reheat for serving. It improves with standing. DO NOT BOIL. Serves 8.

NEW ENGLAND FISH CHOWDER

4 slices salt pork, diced
1 med. onion, minced
2 large potatoes, diced
2 lbs. pollack, cod, or
haddock fillets
1 pt. milk
Butter
Salt and pepper to taste
½ tsp. sugar
½ tsp. basil

Fry out salt pork in heavy skillet until golden brown, add minced onion and sauté until transparent. Add potatoes and just enough water to cover, and cook until potatoes are nearly done. Cut fish in large pieces and place on top, sprinkle with basil, salt, pepper and sugar. Cover and cook until fish flakes—about 10 minutes. Add milk, stir gently. Add walnut size piece of butter and serve piping hot. Serves 8.

FRENCH QUARTER SEAFOOD MELANGE
(Super over baked fillets or spooned over asparagus or broccoli)

¼ lb. cooked shrimp
¼ lb. raw cut up scallops
¼ lb. crab meat
1 can chopped or minced clams
1 small onion chopped
2 sticks celery chopped
1 tsp. chopped parsley
½ tsp. fish seasoning
Salt and pepper to taste
1 cup heavy white sauce
1 tsp. Angostura Bitters (optional)

Sauté onion and celery in a little butter until transparent (do not brown), add seafood (undrained), simmer gently 5-10 minutes. Add herbs and seasonings. Simmer 5 more minutes, let stand while you make white sauce (I use Durkee's packaged White Sauce). Add seafood mix gradually to sauce, let stand uncovered or lightly covered, add Bitters just before serving. Improves with standing if properly refrigerated.

LOBSTER BISQUE
(Old New England Recipe)

¼ cup butter
¼ cup flour
1 tsp. salt
⅛ tsp. pepper
5 cups chicken bouillon
½ cup minced onion
⅓ cup minced carrot
1 leek (white part only,
  minced) if available
1 bay leaf
2 cooked chicken lobsters or
3 5-oz. cans drained lobster
2 egg yolks
1 cup cream

Melt butter in deep kettle, blend in flour, salt and pepper; gradually stir in bouillon. When bubbling add onion, carrot, leek, and bay leaf. Cover and simmer over low heat 10 minutes. Finely mince lobster meat, reserving a few large pieces for garnish. Stir minced lobster into soup, cover and simmer 10 minutes longer. Remove bay leaf. Slightly beat egg yolks and add to soup, stirring vigorously until blended. Simmer 5 minutes more, stirring all the time—DO NOT BOIL. Gradually stir in 1 cup of cream. Add large pieces of lobster and serve piping hot. Serves 6.

SHRIMP STEW

2 med. onions chopped
1 cup sliced fresh mushrooms
1 tbsp. butter
2 cups milk
2 cups water
2 tbsps. instant potatoes
½ lb. cooked shrimp
½ tsp. salt
⅛ tsp. pepper
2 dashes Worcestershire sauce

Sauté onions and mushrooms in butter until onions are transparent. Stir in milk, water, shrimp, instant potato, salt, pepper, and Worcestershire sauce. Heat to steaming—DO NOT BOIL. Makes 4-6 cups.

ESCOFFIER CLAM BROTH
(Canada)

3 doz. cherrystone clams in shell
4 shallots minced
3 tbsps. fresh parsley minced
2 tbsps. olive oil

Wash and scrub clams and place in 3 cups of water. Add shallots, parsley, and sprinkle with olive oil. Cover tightly and steam until clams open. Let stand until sediment settles. Strain broth, reheat, and add a few whole clams to each serving. Serves 6.

DIPS

SAUCES

AND

MARINADES

POPOBIANCO
(Clam Sauce–Providence, Rhode Island)

1 qt. of clams in shell
1 med. onion, sliced
1 cup of white wine
½ cup olive oil
3 cloves garlic, whole
½ cup chopped parsley
¼ tsp. basil
Salt and pepper to taste
1 stalk celery coarsely cut

Wash clams thoroughly removing all sand from shells with brush if necessary. Put them in large kettle with onion, celery, and wine. Cover tightly and steam until clams open (approximately 8-10 minutes). Remove clams from shell and strain broth. Heat olive oil with garlic, parsley, basil, and seasoning. Reduce broth by ½ and add to oil mixture and let just come to boil. Remove garlic cloves and add chopped clams. Serve over thin spaghetti. Serves 2-4.

COURT BOUILLON

¾ cup milk
¾ cup water
½ tsp. salt

Combine and use for poaching 2 steaks or 4 fillets of steak. Increase evenly for larger amounts of fish to be poached.

PARSLEY BUTTER
(Moi)

½ cup butter
½ tsp. salt
Dash black pepper
½ tsp. parsley
1 tbsp. lemon juice

Mix all ingredients and let stand in refrigerator.

ANCHOVY DIP and CELERY CURLS

2 2-oz. cans anchovy fillets
1 clove garlic, pressed
3 tbsps. vinegar
1½ tbsps. salad oil
Chilled celery curls

Rinse anchovies in water, drain and mix with other ingredients. Pour over celery curls, chill.

LOUISIANA RÉMOULADE SAUCE

3 tbsps. horseradish
½ cup hot mustard
3 cloves garlic crushed
1 large onion chopped
1 stalk celery finely chopped
2 tbsps. paprika
4 sprigs parsley chopped
1 cup salad oil
Salt and pepper to taste
1 oz. Worcestershire sauce

Combine all ingredients. Allow to marinate for 12 or more hours before using. Serve over boiled shrimp, crab meat, or flaked fish, on shredded lettuce as an appetizer.

SEAFOOD MARINADES

1 clove garlic minced
1 scallion minced
1 tsp. lemon juice
4 dashes Tabasco
1 cup flour
2 cups water
1 egg yolk beaten
1 tsp. salt
¼ tsp. fresh ground black
pepper
2 egg whites
1 cup cooked diced shrimp,
lobster, or shredded crab meat
(may also use chicken or
turkey)

Pound to a paste the garlic, scallion, lemon juice, and Tabasco. Mix the flour and water until smooth. Beat in egg yolk and salt and pepper, then the paste. Chill for 30 minutes. Beat the egg whites until stiff but not dry, and fold into the batter. Fold in the selected ingredients. Heat oil to 390 degrees and drop teaspoons of mixture into it and cook 2 minutes. Must be golden brown—but do not overcook.

SAUCY SHRIMP DIP

½ tsp. horseradish
2 tsps. sugar
2 tsps. vinegar
4 tbsps. soy sauce

Mix all ingredients and chill 1-2 hours. Makes ¼ cup. Increase evenly for quantity serving.

NEWBURG SAUCE

1 qt. light cream
1 pt. whole milk
¾ cup butter or margarine
¾ cup flour
1 tbsp. paprika
⅓ cup sherry
1 drop Tabasco
Salt to taste

Heat butter in heavy saucepan until bubbles form. Add paprika and flour and mix well. Add scalded cream and milk ⅓ at a time, mixing well after each addition. Add sherry slowly while stirring, add salt and Tabasco and adjust flavoring to taste. Makes 1½ quarts of medium thick sauce which can be frozen and kept for future use.

MUSTARD SAUCE

¾ cup prepared mustard
1 tbsp. steak sauce–A-1
1 tbsp. vinegar
1 tbsp. lemon juice
1 packet instant chicken broth mix
1 packet instant beef broth mix
Dash Angostura Bitters

Combine all ingredients and chill. Makes 1 cup.

LINGUINE CLAM SAUCE
(North End, Boston, Massachusetts)

1 qt. tomato juice
1 can tomato paste
½ cup wine vinegar
¼ tsp. sage leaves
¼ tsp. oregano
½ tsp. coarsely ground black pepper
¼ tsp. basil
¼ tsp. garlic salt
1 small bay leaf
3 cups shucked clams with shell juice

Combine all ingredients except clams in an iron kettle or saucepan. Simmer uncovered over moderate heat until tomato sauce is reduced by half. Add clams and their juice. Simmer an additional 5 minutes. Serve over linguine. Serves 4.

VINHA D'ALHOES
(Portuguese fish or seafood marinade)

1 cup vinegar
3 cups water
2 garlic cloves, minced
1 tsp. salt
½ tsp. black pepper
Pinch of cumin seed

Mix all together and let stand. Excellent for marinating meats also.

MARINADE SAUCE

¼ cup salad oil
¼ cup soy sauce
2 tbsps. catsup
1 tbsp. herb vinegar
¼ tsp. pepper
2 cloves garlic crushed

Mix all together and let
stand—the longer the better.

SHRIMP COCKTAIL SAUCE
(Narragansett Pier, Rhode Island)

1 tbsp. horseradish
½ cup tomato catsup
6 tbsps. lemon juice
3 drops Tabasco sauce
⅛ tsp. salt
½ tsp. celery salt

Blend all ingredients together and
chill well before serving.

TUNA DIP
(Canada)

1 18-oz. pkg. cream cheese, softened
2 tbsps. crumbled bleu cheese
1 6½-oz. can tuna, drained
½ cup soured cream
2 tsps. minced onion
1 whole can pimentos, cut up
1 tbsp. lemon juice
1 tbsp. water

Place all ingredients in blender. Turn to high for 30 seconds. Chill for several hours. Serve with crackers or potato chips. Makes 2 cups.

SHRIMPLY DIVINE DIP
(Moi)

1 3-oz. pkg. of cream cheese, softened
1 cup of soured cream
½ lb. cooked shrimp
1 ⅝-oz. pkg. of Italian dressing mix
2 tsps. lemon juice

Blend all ingredients except shrimp and chill 1 hour or more. Place in container in middle of large plate, place shrimp around on crushed ice and serve as appetizer. Serves 4.

RÉMOULADE CRAB MEAT DIP
(Tina's)

½ lb. king crab, flaked
1 tsp. English mustard
2 hard cooked eggs, sieved
8 chopped green olives
1 tbsp. lemon juice
1 pressed garlic bud
2 tsps. Tabasco
½ cup mayonnaise
Salt to taste

Mix all ingredients together thoroughly. Cover. Let marinate overnight in refrigerator. When ready to serve turn into small chilled dish garnished with fresh parsley and strips of pimento. Serve with plain crackers.

MINT SAUCE
(Mother's)

⅓ cup mint, chopped
2 tbsps. sugar
½ cup hot vinegar

Mix together and stir until sugar is dissolved.

SAUCE CAPER
(Moi)

1½ tbsps. butter
1½ tbsps. flour
1 cup chicken bouillon
1 tsp. lemon juice
1 tsp. salt
Pepper to taste
½ cup capers, drained

Melt butter gently, add flour to paste, stir in bouillon until slightly thickened, add all other ingredients and let cool. Improves with standing.

BUTTER CLAM SAUCE

¼ lb. butter
2 garlic cloves, finely chopped
¼ cup shallots, finely chopped
1 7-oz. can minced clams
¼ cup chopped parsley

Melt butter in a heavy skillet. Sauté garlic and shallots until golden. Add parsley and the entire contents of canned clams. Bring to a hard boil for 3 minutes. Increase according to need. Serves 4.

CUCUMBER SAUCE
(Excellent with fish loaves)

¼ cup Miracle Whip
½ cup dairy sour cream
¼ cup chopped cucumber

Mix all ingredients and refrigerate. Dash of Angostura Bitters is delightful!

MARINARA SAUCE
(Nina's)

1 cup sliced mushrooms
2 cups tomato juice
1 tbsp. minced onions
1 tbsp. parsley flakes
½ tsp. basil
⅛ tsp. oregano

Combine all ingredients in saucepan. Simmer until mixture is reduced by half. Makes 2 cups.

TART SAUCE

1 cup boiling water
2 chicken bouillon cubes
1 2-oz. jar sliced pimentos

Crumble cubes in water, dissolve and let cool. Puree pimentos with fork and add. Chill. Makes 1¼ cups.

MISCELLANEOUS
SEAFOOD
DISHES

ARTHUR'S BACKYARD NEW ENGLANDER

1 chicken lobster per person
20 clams per person
1 pkg. fresh carrots
1 ear corn per person
Water
12" squares heavy duty
aluminum foil

Place live lobsters in refrigerator for 3 hours. Wash shellfish and prepare vegetables, cutting carrots in strips, shuck corn and save inside husks. Line squares of foil with corn husks (seaweed is better if available). Place 10 clams on each piece of foil, ½ lobster on 1 piece of foil, corn and carrots on 1 piece of foil, fold up edges and pour 1 cup of water on shellfish and ½ cup over corn and carrots. Double seal packets and place on red hot charcoal or bake in oven at 375 degrees for 25 minutes. Serve with Perkins Cove broth. (See opposite page)

PERKINS COVE BROTH
(Perkins Cove, Maine)

1 cup clam juice
1 cup chicken bouillon
1 tbsp. butter
1 tsp. celery salt
½ tsp. onion powder
1 tsp. paprika

Simmer all together, let stand, and reheat when ready to serve.

CRAB À LA KING
(Baltimore)

¼ cup chopped green pepper
1 tsp. minced onions
2 tbsps. butter
¼ cup flour
1½ cup milk
½ lb. crab meat, fresh or frozen
1 can or ¼ lb. fresh sautéed mushrooms
¼ cup chopped pimento
¼ tsp. salt
¼ tsp. paprika
Pepper to taste

In a skillet, cook green peppers and onions in butter until just tender, stirring frequently. Blend in flour gradually; stir in milk. Cook until thick, but DO NOT BOIL. Add crab, mushrooms, pimento, and seasonings. Heat thoroughly, keep warm over hot water. Serve in pastry shells or over toast points. Serves 6.

BOUILLABAISSE
(French Quarter, New Orleans)

1 chicken bouillon cube
1 beef broth cube
2 cups water
1 cup clam juice
1 cup tomato juice
1 tbsp. lemon juice
2 tbsps. parsley flakes
2 tbsps. onion flakes
1 halibut steak
1/4 cup green pepper chopped
1/4 tsp. thyme
2 bay leaves
1/2 tsp. allspice
1 pinch saffron
8 oz. of okra
12-oz. can red snapper
1/2 lb. cooked shrimp

Combine bouillon, broth mix, and water in saucepan. Bring just to boil. Reduce heat and add clam juice, tomato juice, lemon juice, parsley flakes, onion flakes, green pepper, thyme, bay leaves, allspice, and saffron. Simmer 10 minutes. Add okra, fish, and shrimp (cut up). Simmer 10 minutes longer. Improves with standing and reheating. Serves 6.

BEACON HILL CRAB CAKES

2 tbsps. chicken bouillon
2 tbsps. minced onions
4 slices dark or cracked
wheat bread, toasted
½ lb. crab meat, fresh or
frozen
1 egg well beaten
1 tsp. dry mustard
1 tsp. salt
1 tsp. paprika

Combine bouillon and onion; roll toast into crumbs, add ¼ of the crumbs to bouillon and mix with crab meat, egg, and seasonings. Shape into 8 equal patties. Roll in remaining crumbs, coating each side equally. Place in a shallow, lightly buttered baking dish and bake at 350 degrees for 30 minutes. Serve with mustard sauce (see sauces). Serves 4.

CRAB MEAT CASSEROLE
(With Cheese Biscuit Toppers)

½ cup shortening
½ cup chopped onions
½ cup sifted flour
1 tsp. dry mustard
½ tsp. seasoned salt
1 cup shredded American
cheese
½ lb. fresh crab meat
(or 1 6½-oz. can, drained)
1 #2 can tomatoes
2 tsps. Worcestershire

Melt shortening in double boiler. Add onions. Cook over boiling water until tender. Blend in flour, mustard, seasoned salt, milk, and cheese. Stir constantly until thick and cheese is all melted. Add crab meat, tomatoes, Worcestershire and blend thoroughly. Pour into a two quart casserole. Place in 350 degree preheated oven to keep warm while preparing Toppers.

Cheese Biscuit Toppers

1 cup flour
½ tsp. salt
2 tbsps. shortening
2 tsps. baking powder
¼ cup shredded American
cheese
½ cup milk

Sift dry ingredients and add cheese. Cut in shortening until mix resembles coarse meal. Add milk and drop by teaspoons on top of crab mixture. Bake 15 to 20 minutes. Serves 6-8.

CRABBY POTATOES
(Moi)

4 even sized baking potatoes
¼ cup butter
2 tsps. Worcestershire sauce
2 tsps. parsley flakes
½ lb. fresh crab meat
½ cup cheddar cheese
Salt and pepper to taste

Bake potatoes at 400 degrees until soft. Cut in half evenly, lengthwise. Carefully remove potato and mash with butter, salt and pepper, Worcestershire sauce, and parsley and whip until fluffy. Fold in crab meat. Fill skins with mixture and top with cheese. Return to oven to melt cheese and serve hot.

CRAB MEAT DREAMS
(Saturday Nite in Padanaram)

8 oz. crab meat cooked and flaked
½ lb. cheddar cheese, grated
1 pimento chopped
1 small onion minced
1 small green pepper chopped
½ cup milk
1 can tomato soup

In top of double boiler combine all ingredients and cook until cheese is melted and sauce is smooth and creamy. Serve piping hot over toasted muffin halves. Serves 4.

CRAB CANAPÉS
(For cocktails)

1 6-oz. can crab meat
drained and flaked
18 slices thin bread—remove
crust
5 tbsps. melted butter
1 8-oz. pkg. cream cheese
¼ cup catsup
1 tsp. grated onion
1 tsp. parsley
½ tsp. Worcestershire sauce

Cut 5 rounds from each slice of bread with a 1¼ inch cookie cutter or glass. Make rings by removing centers with ¾ inch cutter. Brush one side of rounds with butter. Place on lightly greased baking sheet with buttered side up. Brush both sides of rings with butter and place one on each round. Bake 6 minutes at 425 degrees. Cool completely. Fill each ring with flaked crab meat. Mix all other ingredients together well and drop a little mound of it on top of crab meat. Garnish with capers and serve. Serves 10-12.

CRAB CANAPÉS
(A favorite of Anne's)

1 can of refrigerated crescent
dinner rolls
1 6-oz. can crab meat
drained and flaked
(or ½ lb. fresh crab meat)
¼ cup chili sauce
⅓ cup dairy sour cream
½ tsp. Worcestershire sauce

Separate dough into 8 triangles. Cut each in 4 small triangles. Combine crab, chili sauce, and Worcestershire sauce. Spread about 1 teaspoon on each triangle. Place on an ungreased cookie sheet. Top with ½ teaspoon of sour cream and bake at 375 degrees for 10-12 minutes until golden brown. Serves 6-8.

CURRY FISH HORS d'OEUVRE
(Tina's)

2 lbs. fish fillets
½ cup onion bouillon
½ tsp. curry powder
Fine bread crumbs, seasoned

Cut fish into bite size pieces and brush with onion bouillon. Mix crumbs and curry powder and cover bits of fish lightly. Bake in shallow pan at 400 degrees for 5 minutes. Serve with toothpicks. Serves 4.

CRAB-MACARONI SALAD
(Janice's)

½ lb. elbow or shell
macaroni
½ cup mayonnaise
¾ cup milk
½ cup French dressing
½ tsp. salt
¼ tsp. pepper
1 cup flaked crab meat (or
lobster)
1 cup thinly sliced celery
2 thinly sliced small white
onions
2 cups finely shredded
cabbage
3 hard cooked eggs sliced
½ cup sliced stuffed olives

Cook macaroni, drain, and run
cold water over it in colander so
it will not be sticky, and chill. In
a large bowl combine
mayonnaise, milk, French
dressing, salt and pepper. Add
chilled macaroni—toss. Add crab
and rest of ingredients, saving
eggs and olives for garnish.
Serves 8.

SALMON QUICHE
(Beaty's)

9" pie crust
1 cup heavy cream
3 eggs
1 cup leftover salmon (or
small can)
½ cup cheddar cheese, grated

Combine eggs, cream, and salmon until well blended. Pour into baked pie crust and sprinkle cheese over top. Bake at 375 degrees for 30 minutes until a knife inserted near the center comes out clean. Serves 6.

SUMMER SALAD ROLLS

2 cups chopped lettuce
1 cup diced cooked fish
½ cup diced processed
American or Swiss cheese
½ cup chopped celery
½ cup mayonnaise
2 tbsps. of pickle relish
¼ tsp. curry powder
(optional)
8 frankfurter rolls, split,
toasted, and buttered

In a medium size bowl combine fish, cheese, and celery. Blend mayonnaise, pickle relish and curry powder. Stir into the first mixture to coat well and pile into prepared rolls. Tuna, shrimp or crab meat may also be used. Serves 8.

CRAB MEAT QUICHE
(Moi)

3 eggs, slightly beaten
1 cup sour cream
½ tsp. Worcestershire sauce
¾ tsp. salt
1 cup coarsely shredded Swiss cheese
½ lb. crab meat, flaked
1 3½-oz. can French fried onions
1 9" baked pastry shell
¼ tsp. Angostura Bitters

Combine eggs, sour cream, Worcestershire sauce, and salt. Stir in cheese, crab meat, and onion. Pour into pastry shell—sprinkle Bitters over top, bake in oven at 375 degrees 45-50 minutes or until custard sets and a knife inserted in center comes out clean. For appetizers, use small pastry shells and cut down cooking time. Serve hot. Serves 8.

RHODE ISLAND CLAM CAKES
(Marie's)

1 6-oz. pkg. Krisppe–Famous
Rhode Island Batter Mix
1 8-oz. can minced
clams–drained (save liquid)
Water
1/8 tsp. cayenne

Add water to clam juice to 2/3 cup of liquid and mix with batter mix, clams, and cayenne, folding gently. Handle as little as possible. Let stand a few minutes and drop by heaping teaspoons into deep hot fat. Use a basket preferably. Remove when golden brown and serve hot or cold. Best hot! Makes 12-16.

MOSSELEN
(Mussels steamed with white wine – Dutch)

2-3 pts. small mussels
1 cup white wine
1/2 cup finely chopped parsley
Salt and pepper to taste
To make a richer dish add 1
cup of heavy cream to broth
before serving.

Let mussels stand in cold water an hour or so. Then scrape and place in colander under running cold water. Drain, place in large kettle or Dutch oven, add wine and cover. Cook over medium heat until mussels open. To the broth add salt and pepper to taste and parsley, and serve in bowls with broth. Serves 4-6.

SCALLOP CASSEROLE
(Betty's)

1 pt. scallops
½ cup melted butter or
margarine
½ cup soft bread crumbs
1 cup Ritz cracker crumbs
⅔ cup evaporated milk
Salt and pepper to taste

In a buttered casserole alternate mixture of cracker crumbs and scallops in that order, drizzling butter over scallops , followed with a little seasoning; end with crumbs and pour evaporated milk over all. Add a few dots of butter here and there and bake at 350 degrees covered, for ½ hour. Remove cover last 10 minutes to bring crumbs to golden brown. Serve piping hot. Serves 4.

SARDINE SANDWICH FILLING

Mash 1 can (3¼-4 oz.) sardines. Mix with 2 hard cooked eggs minced, ¼ cup finely diced celèry, 3 tablespoons mayonnaise, 1 teaspoon lemon juice, salt and pepper to taste.

RUM-TUM-TIDDY
(Boothbay Harbor, Maine)

1 tbsp. butter
1 can condensed tomato soup
¾ cup milk
¾ lb. shredded Cheddar cheese
½ tsp. Worcestershire sauce
¼ cup onion–chopped
¼ cup green pepper–chopped
1 egg beaten slightly
¼ cup sherry
½ lb. flaked crab meat

Melt butter over moderate heat and add onion and pepper. Cook until tender. Remove from heat. Mix in soup, milk, cheese, Worcestershire sauce, and simmer over low heat, stirring constantly until cheese melts. Blend ½ cup of this sauce into beaten egg and blend all together. Add sherry and serve piping hot over toast or crackers. Shrimp, lobster, tuna, or any leftover fish may be substituted. Serves 6.

SALMON PARTY LOG

1 1-lb. can (2 cups) salmon
1 8-oz. pkg. cream cheese
softened
1 tbsp. lemon juice
2 tsps. grated onion
1 tsp. prepared horseradish
¼ tsp. salt
¼ tsp. liquid smoke
½ cup chopped pecans
2 tbsps. chopped parsley

Drain and flake salmon, removing skin and bones. Combine salmon with next 6 ingredients and mix thoroughly. Chill several hours. Combine pecans and parsley. Shape salmon mixture in 8 inch x 2 inch log; roll in nut mixture, chill well. Serve with crackers. Serves 6-8.

TEEN-TUNA
(A favorite with the youngsters)

8 slices of bread
16 oz. drained and flaked
tuna
½ cup chopped pimentos
3 tbsps. minced onions
3 tbsps. parsley flakes
2 tbsps. lemon juice
¼ cup mustard
¼ cup mayonnaise

Remove crust from bread and flatten well with rolling pin. Form open roll and secure sides with toothpicks. Bake at 500 degrees until golden brown. Mix tuna fish with all other ingredients, blending well. Spoon in equal portions in toast boats and serve. Serves 8.

CRABBY ONIONS
(Moi)

6 med. yellow onions
6 oz. cooked crab meat
1 tsp. parsley flakes
½ tsp. lemon juice
Bread crumbs
Salt and pepper to taste
Paprika
2 tbsps. butter

Pour boiling water over onions, skin and core, leaving ½ inch shells. Chop up onions and sauté quickly in butter until ALMOST tender. Cook shells in boiling water until ALMOST tender. Mix flaked crab meat with cores and seasonings with just enough crumbs to hold together. Fill shells and sprinkle tops with a few crumbs and paprika. Pour one can of chicken consomme around them and bake at 350 degrees for 20 minutes or until lightly brown and tender when pierced with a fork. Serves 6.

FISH TURBOT
(Cape Cod, Massachusetts)

3 lbs. haddock steaks,
skinned and boned
¼ cup white wine (optional)
1½ cup white sauce
2 eggs hard-boiled, sieved
1 small onion chopped
1 tsp. parsley
Fine seasoned bread crumbs
Salt and pepper to taste

Steam fish until it can be flaked. Cut into bite-size pieces and place in lightly buttered casserole. Mix white sauce, and add onion and parsley with sieved egg to it and pour over fish. Sprinkle wine over all, then sprinkle with bread crumbs. Bake for 30 minutes at 350 degrees, or until golden brown. Serves 10-12.

YUMMY SHRIMP SALAD SANDWICH
(Mickey Baine's, Nashville, Tennessee)

*1 cup of fresh shrimp, cooked
and chopped
½ cup diced celery
Salt and pepper to taste
Few drops herb vinegar
Russian dressing
8 whole wheat rolls
Lettuce
Butter
1 egg, hard-cooked and
chopped*

Mix shrimp, celery, and seasonings together. Moisten with a few drops of vinegar. Then mix with enough dressing to just hold together. Split and butter the rolls. Place a piece of crisp lettuce on each roll, spread on a large spoonful of salad mixture and sprinkle with chopped egg. Serves 8.

CREAMED FRESH HADDOCK
(County Cork, Ireland)

8 fresh haddock fillets
1 cup light cream
½ cup melted butter
1 heaping tsp. English
mustard
Flour
Salt and pepper to taste

Season flour with salt and pepper and roll fillets in it, then roll in melted butter. Put them in a flat pan with any leftover butter and add cream. Heat gently and when it starts to bubble, reduce flame, cover and simmer very gently for 10-15 minutes more until liquid is reduced. Remove to a warm serving dish and keep hot. Stir mustard in remaining sauce and reduce further until slightly thickened. Pour over fish and serve. Other fillets such as cod, hake, etc. may be used with this recipe. Serves 8.

HALIBUT SOUFFLÉ
(Freda's)

1½ lbs. halibut fillet
1½ cups soft bread crumbs
1 cup hot milk
1 tsp. baking powder
1 tsp. celery salt
⅛ tsp. cayenne
1 pimento minced
Salt and pepper to taste
2 egg whites beaten stiff

Boil fillets in small amount of water until you can flake with fork (4-5 minutes). Flake fish and add to paste made with bread and milk; add baking powder, celery salt, salt, pepper, and pimento and mix well. Fold in beaten egg whites, bake in greased baking dish lined with waxed paper—put dish in pan of water and bake at 350 degrees for 45 minutes. Serves 4-6.

CRAB CANAPÉ
(Moi)

*1 8-oz. can of crab meat, or
8 oz. fresh, shredded
1 pkg. sharp cheddar cheese
1 tsp. Worcestershire sauce
1 small onion, minced
1 loaf very thin bread
(remove crust)*

Drain, clean, and crumble crab meat. Break cheese into small pieces in top of double boiler and when melted add crab, onion, and Worcestershire sauce. Mix well. Toast slices of bread lightly and cut in four pieces. Cover each piece with mixture and put under broiler 3-4 minutes until bubbly and golden. Delicious hot or cold. Serves 6-8.

DEEP-FRIED CRAB CAKES
(New Orleans)

2 tbsps. butter	Cook onion in butter until
2 tbsps. minced onion	transparent. Add bread crumbs,
3 cups bread crumbs	crab meat, egg, seasonings. Shape
1 lb. crab meat—fresh or	into cakes. Coat with extra
frozen	crumbs. Deep-fry at 375 degrees
1 well beaten egg	until they float, about 3-7
1 tsp. parsley	minutes. Serve with tartar sauce.
1/4 tsp. each of salt and	For hors d'oeuvres, shape into
paprika	small balls. Serves 6-8.

PIGS IN BLANKETS
(Moi)

Season large oysters with salt and pepper. Cut slices of bacon in half.
Wrap an oyster in each half and fasten with a toothpick. Run under
broiler to crisp bacon—watching constantly—overcooking will be
disastrous. Serve with saffron rice and tossed green salad.

COD'S ROE RAMEKINS
(Traditional Irish breakfast)

½ lb. cooked cod roe
2 cups loosely packed bread
crumbs
2 eggs separated
Pinch of mace
¼ cup cream
Juice of ½ lemon
1 tbsp. chopped parsley
Salt and pepper to taste

Do not choose too large a roe—the smaller ones have more flavor. Wrap in a piece of cheese cloth and cook *very* gently in salted water for at least 30 minutes. Take out and chill. Remove membrane before using.

Mash roe, crumbs, and seasonings, add lemon juice and egg yolks beaten with cream. Let set 10 minutes then add stiffly beaten egg whites. Put into greased individual dishes or one large baking dish and bake at 400 degrees until golden brown and puffed up. Serves 4.

POACHED SHAD ROE
(Moi)

2 pairs roe
¼ cup butter
¼ cup bacon drippings
1 tbsp. dried parsley
6 strips of bacon crisped
Juice of 1 lemon
½ tsp. pepper

Crisp bacon and remove from pan. Handle roe *very* gently so as not to puncture. Heat butter and bacon drippings adding parsley and lemon juice. Place roe in pan, cover and cook, using moderate heat for 10 minutes on each side—turn very carefully. Place on hot platter, sprinkle with crumbled bacon and garnish with fresh parsley and sliced lemon. Serves 4.

LOBSTER ROLLS
(Moi)

¼ lb. butter
½ lb. cheddar cheese
1 lb. lobster meat, fresh or
frozen
2 loaves very fresh sliced
white bread

Melt butter and cheese together in double boiler. Add lobster meat. Remove crusts from white bread. Roll each slice very thin with rolling pin. Spread lobster mixture on bread slices. Roll up in waxed paper and freeze. When ready to serve, cut each roll in half and spread with a little additional butter. Defrost and bake at 400 degrees for 10 minutes or until slightly golden. Cooked fresh mushrooms may also be substituted for lobster meat for another delicious hors d'oeuvre.

MAVERICK CLAMS

36 *cherrystone clams*
8 *tbsps. finely chopped green*
pepper
2 *tbsps. finely chopped*
pimento
1 *tbsp. capers*
1 *tbsp. chives*
1 *tsp. Worcestershire sauce*

Arrange clams on the ½ shell or in a shallow baking dish. Combine all other ingredients and place a scant teaspoon of mixture on each clam. Broil 3 inches from unit for 5 minutes. Serve at once. Makes 6-8 servings.

ELLA'S ESCALLOPED QUAHOGS
(South Dartmouth, Massachusetts)

1 *pt. cutout quahogs*
(save liquid in shells when
opening)
1 *cup milk*
1 *egg*
¼ *tsp. pepper*
Uneeda Biscuits, coarsely
crumbled

Beat milk, egg, and pepper together and add liquid from quahogs. Alternate layers of cracker crumbs and quahogs, ending with crumbs. Make holes down through the layers with a fork. Pour liquid mixture over all. Dot with butter generously and bake in 325 degree oven for 1 hour. Serves 4.

SALMON LOAF

Combine a 1 pound can of salmon, drained and flaked, with ½ cup of Miracle Whip, 1 can of condensed cream of celery soup, 1 beaten egg, 1 cup of dry bread crumbs, ½ cup of chopped onion, 1 tablespoon of lemon juice, 1 teaspoon of salt. Bake in greased 8½ x 4½ inch loaf pan at 350 degrees for 1 hour. Serve with Cucumber Sauce (see sauces). Serves 8.

HOT 'N HEARTY
(He-man special!)

1 pkg. cooked frozen peas
(reserve ¼ cup liquid)
2 7-oz. cans tuna
1 small can pimento, chopped
1 small can sliced mushrooms
(save ¼ cup juice)
1 med. onion, minced
½ cup mayonnaise
1 tbsp. flour
¼ tsp. salt
Dash pepper
Dash garlic salt

Toss all together lightly and bake in greased covered casserole in moderate oven 375 degrees for 20 minutes. Serve with noodles, rice, macaroni or toast. Delicious also with salmon, crab meat or lobster. Serves 6.

TUNA SAVANNAH
(Nanna's)

1 cup tuna
3 tbsps. chopped onion
1 10½-oz. can condensed
tomato soup
½ cup water
1 tsp. chili powder
1 tsp. salt
1 tsp. Worcestershire sauce
1½ cups cooked noodles
1 cup grated American cheese

Melt butter, add onion and cook slowly until transparent. Add soup, water, and seasonings. Simmer 5 minutes. Combine sauce with noodles, cheese, and tuna. Put into greased 1 quart casserole and bake at 350 degrees for 30 minutes. Serves 4.

QUAHOG POPOVERS
(Cape Cod, Massachusetts)

6 med. quahogs–steam open
and chop up
2 eggs
1 cup liquid–½ milk, ½
quahog liquid
1 tbsp. melted butter
1 cup all-purpose flour
Pepper and salt to taste

Thoroughly blend eggs, milk, quahog liquid, and melted butter in mixing bowl, beating gently. Gradually add flour and seasoning, then quahogs, mix thoroughly.

Have ready small ovenware cups heated and greased with butter. Fill half full and bake at 350 degrees for approximately 45 minutes, until they have popped and turned brown. Serve immediately—cut in four pieces with a dot of butter and a drop of lemon juice on each piece.

GAELIC PATÉ
(Ireland)

½ lb. smoked salmon
2 oz. butter
1 tbsp. olive oil
½ tbsp. lemon juice
4 tbsps. heavy cream
Pinch cayenne pepper
1 tsp. whiskey (optional)

Mince the salmon finely. Place the butter and olive oil in a mixing bowl and cream thoroughly. Gradually beat in smoked salmon to make a smooth paste. Beat in lemon juice, cream, cayenne pepper, and spirits. Pile into a small serving pot and chill. Serve with thinly sliced whole wheat bread, buttered, as an appetizer. Serves 4-6.

HURRY-UP NEWBURG
(Cooking with your hat on!)

1 envelope French's white sauce
1 envelope French's cheese sauce
1 can frozen shrimp soup, undiluted
1 pimento, chopped
½ lb. fresh crab meat, shredded
½ lb. fresh shrimp, cut up (2 cans crab meat and 1 can shrimp may be substituted)
¼ cup sherry

Prepare sauce mixes according to package directions. Mix all ingredients together in top of double boiler and heat. Serve in patty shells. Serves 6-8.

INDEX

NOTES FOR COOKS